Eve's Eyes

Women Have Rights Because…

Eve's Eyes

Women Have Rights Because...

ANOINTED ROSE PRESS™

ANOINTED ROSE PRESS™

The Anointed Rose Press name and logo are registered Trademarks
ANOINTED ROSE PRESS™ PUBLISHING

Eve's Eyes©
Women Have Rights Because...

SEPTEMBER SUMMER
Email: septembersummer09@gmail.com
Website: www.september-summer.com

ISBN-13: 9780982684122
ISBN-10: 0-98266841-2-6
©2014 by September Summer

Anointed Rose Press
Coatesville, PA 19320
Email: anointed.rose.press@gmail.com

Library of Congress Control Number: 2014935458
Library of Congress Catalog-in-Publication Data

Summer, September
Eve's Eyes / September Summer
p.cm.

ISBN 0-98266841-2-6 (trade pbk.: alk. Paper)

08 09 10 11 12 13 14   AnR LS   10 9 8 7 6 5 4 3 2 1

1.Religion:Christian Life-Women's Issues 2. Family & Relationships: General

Cover Design:
ANOINTED ROSE PRESS
Coatesville, PA (267) 428-1721

Printed in the USA for worldwide distribution.
May not be reproduced or transmitted for commercial purposes, except for brief quotations in printing, without permission from the publisher

Dedication

I dedicate this publication to women

in all the

various corners of the world,

to those

who have gone before us

and to

those who come after

...to all

the daughters of Eve.

You are a glory to behold, and still are soooo precious in the eyes of our Creator.

...September

Acknowledgments

I give the highest Praise, Glory and Honor to my Heavenly Father, who loves me with unconditional love and grace. Thank you.

I am so thankful for my parents, my awesome children, and each of my next two generations that are with us. How amazingly we are blessed!!

Thank you to all of my friends, loved ones, prayerful supporters and ministry colleagues.

Thank you to all of my GDC church family of Coatesville, PA. Special mention to my wonderful church sisters – I appreciate each of you!!

Last, but definitely not least, I truly thank God for my spiritual covering, Apostle Bobby G. Duncan of Coatesville, PA, a man of much Godly wisdom; and my precious mentor (sister, friend), Rev. Dr. M. Frances Manning-Fontaine of Hackensack, NJ. They have surely lifted my arms up again and again. Godly leadership is invaluable!!

...September

Foreword

From "Can we talk?" to "Can trust be rebuilt?" this book is a how-to on doing relationship at its fullest, finest and most flavorful. I say flavorful because we often say we are blessed and highly "favored"; but I say we are blessed and highly flavored. Flavored through life's experiences, flavored through the travails and trials through which God brings us...travails and trials through life experiences that make us laugh, pray, question, wonder, cry, shout, kick, scream, and holler through the vicissitudes of life through which we come.

This book is filled with conscious conversations. Conversations in which it is clear the author has dialogued with God and others...conversations that are remarkable in their ability to cause us to dialogue with ourselves and God...to teach us...to bring us to that place of grace where we can say that we, too' have been highly flavored by sitting at September Summer's "beautiful" feet. My husband and I are grateful for her wisdom that has "saved" us many times!

Where was she when we needed her? Sitting at the Father's feet for such a time as this! Happy relating!

Aleuta Continua

Dr. M. Frances Manning-Fontaine
Senior Pastor-Teacher

New Hope Baptist Church, Hackensack, New Jersey
Spiritual Advisor
North Jersey District Missionary Baptist Association
Author of **Women With Wind In Their Wings**
(amazon.com)

Foreword

"So God created human beings in his own image. In the image of God he created them; male and female he created them. Then God blessed them and said, "Be fruitful and multiply..." Genesis 1: 27-28 (NLT)

From the beginning, women were a part of God's creation plan. Just reading in Genesis that women were made in his likeness gives me chills. *"I am woman, hear me roar."* Seriously, how proud are we as women for who we are in God.

With that read and said, what a pleasure to have the well-read author, September Summer amplify the importance, impact, and impressions that women especially make in today's society. *"Eve's Eyes", Women Have Rights Because...* opens our eyes to a kaleidoscope of views of how we as women see our own selves, warts and all. The fascinating observations of our "truths" as seen through our eyes will have you wondering, "How did she know I felt or thought that way?"

You will not find any lopsided, male bashing in this frank and honest book of thoughtful observations, but only a curious mind that has put great intuitive points of clarity to paper.

One thing is for certain, September Summer's latest page turner will have you waiting anxiously for the sequel, to answer some other of life's mysterious queries. Please don't keep us waiting too long. We will look forward to your candor and insight; and please don't forget that balanced note of humor. May you continue to share your God-given talent with those who appreciate a quality read when we see on?

Bishop Doris Ford, *Founder, Author*
Cathedral of Faith International Fellowship of Churches and Ministries, Philadelphia, Pennsylvania

Table of Contents

Dedication	vii
Acknowledgements	viii
Foreword	ix
Foreword	x
Table of Contents	xi
Preface	xiii
Introduction	xv

PART ONE — DIFFERENCES…REAL OR FALSE?

Chapter			
	1	Can We Talk	2
	2	How Different Are We?	10
	3	Genetics	17
	4	"Man" at Creation	22
	5	"Male" at Creation	31
	6	"Female" at Creation	34
	7	Are We Incompatible?	40
	8	Help Meet or Floor Mat?	50
	9	Who is She, Anyway?	66
	10	Intuition and Influence	73

PART TWO — WOMEN'S WISDOM

Chapter			
	11	The Heart That Keeps Giving	82
	12	Healing Through Forgiveness	88
	13	Emotions- Not A Female Thang	95

Table of Contents (continued)

PART THREE — MEN SPEAK

Chapter	14	Not Right Now	108
	15	Wish Women Understood	115
	16	Can Trust Be Rebuilt?	121

ABOUT THE AUTHOR   124

OTHER BOOKS BY AUTHOR   125

APPENDIX

	A	Types of Love	127
	B	Relationships/Spice of Life	129
	C	Relationship Building	137
	D	Knapp's Relational Developmental Model	143
	E	Stages of Committed Relationships	149
	F	Sexuality and Spirituality	154
	G	Anger	161
	H	Communication - Can You Hear Me Now?	177
	I	Sexual Development for Teens	180

RECOMMENDED READING/RESOURCES   194

Preface

"...And thy desire shall be unto thy husband, and he shall rule over thee." Gen 3:16

For eons, women have felt the need to have our various 'rights' spoken for. There have been many forms of protest or resistance, ranging from the housewife who let the bread burn on purpose, to the organized marches in front of legislative bodies. In some ways, we can say, "We've come a long way, baby."

It's one thing to say you have a right to something. However, it's a horse of another color (so to speak) to be absolutely confident in yourself that it's true. Secondly, you have to be able to show validation of your claim.

I could walk up to any bank teller and state that I have a right to a million dollars of the money in the bank. But, if I don't possess a certified check or other legal document to prove my claim, I will be laughed at or possibly arrested.

Metaphorically speaking, women's claims to "equal rights" have historically been "sneered at" by societies at large or we have simply been *"arrested"* – *placed under home arrest, abused, denigrated or ignored.*

This isn't a research thesis or a panacea to solve all of the issues between women, our significant others, and the world around us. Nor is it meant to be a "How to get my share of the pie." guidebook.

The focus of "Eve's Eyes" is to address how (1) we often "see" ourselves as females, and (2) how we are generally viewed by many of our counterparts. I present my frank and honest understanding of the general mindset of many "modern" women. Ironically, women of every socio-economic status, ethnicity, culture or spiritual ideology have had many of the same issues throughout history.

I believe in the validity of the Bible. This, in turn, has a major impact upon my worldview. Accordingly, we as women are definitely, "A precious gift" given to the world, by God. It's time for women and men, alike, to have our vision adjusted to see just how extraordinary females are, and that we are truly "fearfully (awesomely) and wonderfully" made. (Psa. 139:14)

...September

Introduction

What gives you the right...?

A major challenge with treating the eye disorder "glaucoma" is that the condition often goes undetected until considerable damage to the optic disc has occurred. Many people have developed varying degrees of irreversible blindness without realizing that their vision was decreasing. The process could be described as the light of vision becoming dim so gradually, that the person doesn't notice until the light is almost gone.

Current technology greatly enhances accurate measurement of the intraocular pressure within the eye during routine exams. This has become the primary mechanism to identify the condition before irreversible damage is done.

A person with healthy eyes may wonder how the affected person could not notice that their vision is gradually being compromised. However, a strange quirk about the human mind and body is that we have the ability to adapt to changes in our environment that occur gradually, positive or negative. Oftentimes, we are not consciously aware that changes are taking place.

Our minds have the amazing, and sometimes unhealthy, capacity to "grow accustomed" to how things are becoming. We can easily lose sight of how things truly should be. You may ask, "What does this line of thinking have to do with this book.

Indeed, there is an increasing societal awareness that how a person "sees" (thinks, believes, perceives) herself is what primarily determines the parameters of who she "considers" herself to be.

This is not to say that what the person "sees" is actually "true" reality; but it is his or her reality. Unless it is somehow detected that a person's vision is distorted, as in glaucoma – the diminished and erroneous "view" is how they will govern their lives.

The impact of this, which people now realize more than ever before, was clearly spelled out in the Bible a very long time ago. The wise man Solomon said in his writings, "For as he thinketh in his heart (mind), so is he..." (Proverbs 23:7) In other words, how we "see" ourselves becomes our reality.

> Unless it is somehow detected that a person's vision is distorted, the erroneous "view" is how they will govern their lives.

As women continue to pursue our "rights" in the various areas of our lives legislatively, socially, economically, and so forth, we must be sure to check our "vision." I propose to you that one of the things that is sorely needed in our current global culture is for us to grasp a "truism" of who we "are" that is accurate and affirming.

We are more than what we are often made to "see" (or believe) about ourselves. We are more than what millions of men have believed about us, down through the centuries. We are more than just silly women; baby Momma's, eyelashes, booties and boobs; although those are definitely part of God's wonderful endowment to us!!

*In the United States, we have "The Declaration of Independence', an historical document which declares, "We hold these truths to be self evident that **all men** are created equal, that they are endowed by their Creator with certain unalienable rights, that among these are Life,*

Liberty and the pursuit of happiness. That to secure these rights, Governments are instituted among men deriving their just powers from the consent of the governed..."[1]

I declare to you that the term "all men" should more properly have been framed "all mankind". Further, I declare that the "rights" that each individual human has, was pre-determined for us by the only being in the entire universe who could legally decide what those rights are. That "being" is the Creator Himself, who made us.

It is my desire that we will "derive the just power" from the consent of our Creator to view ourselves through His eyes, so that we can be healed of our "glaucoma" stricken vision. Then, we can find the answers to our questions – what, who, why am I here?

When I think about what I believe women have desired down through the ages, it's really not too complex. We desire to be treated with love and consideration by our husbands, children, and others who we live in contact with, and to be able to flourish where we are.

---

[1] http://www.ushistory.org/declaration/document

Just as there are a myriad of many different beautiful flowers which have been handcrafted by God, so has He personally handcrafted the female. We adorn the world with our beautiful skin colors in the many hues of Black, Brown, Beige, White, Pink, Red, Yellow, Tan and Olive. Our bodies range from size xx-small to super plus; with a plethora of shapes, from lean to curvy, to hourglass, to Coca Cola bottle, 2-liter bottle, to busty to hippy, to full, to less, and on and on. Hallelujah for the garden!!

We have such an awesome array of personalities and communication styles including introverts, and extroverts, and verbose, and pensive, and soft spoken, and assertive, and hyperactive, and slow rolling, and so forth.

Who else can be so creative with straight hair or kinky hair or short hair or long hair or weaved hair or natural hair or permed hair or curled hair or braided hair or dyed hair, and then make a complete about face in one day?

The flowers are so varied that we have athletes and teachers, and leaders, and followers, and entrepreneurs, and home builders (aka housewives), and fashion designers, and gourmet chefs, and still we are all females.

When we say we have "rights", I believe most of us are simply saying, "I am unique, and when I am allowed to experience love and sunlight and warmth and care and protection and affection, our whole world becomes a more blessed and better place."

Yes, we know that Eve ate the "poison" fruit, and then shared it with Adam, but did that make her a "doomed vixen from that day forward?" I think not.

As the saying goes, "The more I come to know; the more I realize just how much I still need to learn." After years of working in both secular and Christian counseling, I understand better that men and women really do see and experience life differently.

At first, I thought that the idea that "women are impossible for men to understand," was just a male contrived theory to justify poor communication between the sexes. I believed this was a culturally accepted poor excuse to rationalize the challenges which occur when a man and woman fail to see things "eye to eye".

However, I know now that it is, in fact, an established truth that men and women "are different." This is not by choice, but by predetermined genetic design. The prerogative belonged solely to the divine creator from the very beginning of human existence. The anatomical differences, i.e., genitalia and who carries babies are only the most obvious distinctions.

There are also other equally gender-driven attributes that are not so obvious to the naked eye. In "Eve's Eyes", I review some of the visible and some less visible, attributes of women - physically, mentally, emotionally and spiritually. How do we experience our world?

We often hear women make statements such as, "I've spent so much time giving up all that I have to everyone else, that I don't have anything left for myself." Or "I don't know who I am anymore, and I need to find myself." or "Why am I even alive?" or "What is my purpose?"

On the surface, these words may seem somewhat selfish and shallow. However, underneath there is a profound and gut-wrenching sobbing that rises from the very core of the woman's heart. The longer I pondered over this, the more I realized that this is not a trivial matter.

In fact, statistics show an ever-increasing number of women who are the initiators of divorce. At the very least, more women are the ones deciding to walk away from marriage, relationship, children, possessions and all that is familiar.

The numbers are climbing steadily higher each year. Oddly enough, this phenomenon is quite unlike the history of women of previous generations. In general, they could not even imagine themselves walking away from the home and family. Things can change.

If you listen closely, you can hear a deafeningly loud, yet blaringly silent, sound of myriads of women who are struggling to be "**recognized**" and "**liberated**".

Ironically enough, immediately following the reverberations of distress, there follows a "cacophony" of confusion caused by the sound of some equally loud and 'poignant' questions.

> In "Eve's Eyes", we discuss some of the visible, and some of the less visible, perspectives of how women have come to "see" and experience our world.

"Recognized as whom...?" "Liberated from what?" "Liberated to do what?"

As many historians can tell you, **"Liberation without proper preparation often leads to anarchy…not true freedom."**

"For God doth know that in the day ye eat thereof, then your eyes shall be opened, and ye shall be as gods, knowing good and evil." …KJV

****

"EVE, 'WHO' ART THOU?"

"I don't know, Why are you asking me? Half the time, I don't know where or who I am."

"Maybe you should ask my husband, my children, my boss, my girlfriends, my Pastor, society, and everybody else."

"I'm hiding from my kids and husband and everybody else. I need a break."

"I can't talk right now. I'm busy being the wife, the Mommy, the nanny, the nurse, the cook, the chauffeur, the tutor, the cleaner, the ironer, the food shopper, the usher, the missionary, the coach, the Facebook police and a few other things which I can't think of right now."

****

Part One

"Differences…Real or False?"

Chapter 1

"Can We Talk?"

To begin with, I first acknowledge that it is not always an easy task to get someone else to hear what you have to say. I don't know about in other cultures, but in the Western culture where I live, there is a noticeable reaction which takes place when a female asks the question, "Can we talk?" First and foremost, the responder's reaction tends to be quite "gender related" – whether female or male.

If it is at a convenient time, nine out of ten women who are asked the above question will become spontaneously receptive, or at least curious. We will kind of lean in to hear what the person asking the question wants to talk about.

A female responder's mind becomes alert, and a kind of light brightens behind the eyes. An expectation arises that there is getting ready to be some type of connection or interaction made with the questioner, even if only briefly.

On the other hand, if the responder is a male, the body language is altogether different. This is true, regardless of his relationship to the female questioner.

I venture to say that 9¾ out of every 10 men instantly shudder and get a kind of glazed look in their eyes, like a deer caught in headlights!

> On the other hand, if you pay close attention to the body language of a male...

Amazingly, it doesn't matter as to whether he's the husband, brother, son, Pastor or next-door neighbor. For many, the eyes get wide, the vein in the neck will start to pulsate, and beads of sweat will suddenly show up, regardless of the outside temperature.

Wise women learn early in life that there is almost "never" really a convenient time to ask a man, "Can we talk?" Don't expect him to sit right down and say, "Sure Honey (Mom, Sis or friend), what would you like to talk about?" However, I dare say, don't let that deter you from making the effort.

Don't get me wrong, I'm not bashing men or saying that there is a problem with "how" men respond to the question. I am very simply giving an example of the truism that there are definitely differences between males and females – some which are innate (inherited) and some which are learned (conditioned by environment).

There have literally been thousands of books which have addressed the differences and/or similarities between men and women, in multiple aspects. These aspects include communication patterns, perception, emotional responses, intuition, analytical responses and others, as well as the most obvious variant of physical anatomy.

For example, I would like to briefly mention three books which I've found to be user friendly and an easy read. Neither of these books need be thought of as research books. They are rather informal in their format, based on the personal experience of the author or persons the author has knowledge of.

1) In 1992, John Gray (*Relationship Counselor*) wrote a book.[2] Much of his

---

[2] Gray, J. *Men Are From Mars, Women Are From Venus: The Classic Guide to Understanding the Opposite Sex.* Harper Collins: New York, 1992

focus was to help couples improve their interpersonal relationships. The way he approached the issue was to talk about how each side views things.

He helped individuals to better comprehend the "how" and "why" of the actions, the feelings and the perception from the perspective of the opposite sex.

One key thing that struck me about this book is the idea that all men are by nature, "like bears". It is totally natural, and women shouldn't take it personal, for them to need "space" from time to time to "hibernate."

This is a time aside (brief or lengthy) without having to communicate with the female, who wants to cuddle and share as soon as he gets home, and the cubs. It's a time of refreshing for him.

Without taking this needed space, he eventually becomes like a grizzly bear, gruff and easily frustrated. Given a little space, under normal circumstances, he will return and be more "human."

2) In 2006, Bishop David Evans (*Pastor, Media Personality*) released an audiotape series, and in 2009 released it as a book.[3] The author's focus was on strengthening the male by enabling him to understand and tap into the full and dynamic potential within him, and to change his perspective of himself. In turn, the woman is also taught how to better understand, support and be supported by her man.

One significant point I took away from this book is that, unlike women, men don't have the constant need of being in frequent contact with the woman to still "feel" in relationship. Men don't need a phone call every few hours to feel safe, wanted and appreciated.

Hence, for the man, running 2 hours late coming in from work, *without a check-in phone call*, doesn't mean he's never coming home again. Neither does it mean that he's dead on the side of the road somewhere.

---

[3] Evans, D. *Dare to Be Called A Man: The Truth Every Man Must Know...And Every Woman Needs To Know About Him.* Putnam: New York, 2009

Likewise, not getting a "nail biting while waiting" phone call until three days after the first date doesn't mean that he didn't like you or didn't enjoy the date. Men just tend to take a longer time before they feel the need to connect again.

3) In 2011, Steve Harvey (*Media Personality, Stand-up Comedian*) released his book.[4] Harvey's primary focus was about the male, but was written to the female. He talked about what men "really" think about love, relationships, intimacy and commitment.

Bottom line, according to Harvey, is that *every* man – whether professional, laborer, baker, preacher, Indian Chief, healthy, sick, deaf, dumb, crippled, blind or crazy - tends to be more driven by the "little head down under" than by the one that sits on his shoulders.

However, and in spite of that drive, a man still has parameters within which he will choose his "wife". Sadly, for many women, his choice is not always the one

---

[4]Harvey, S. *Act Like A Lady, Think Like A Man: What Men Really Think About Love, Relationships, Intimacy and Commitment*. Amistad: Kansas, 2011

with whom he has prematurely shared the "little head." Even sadder for most women, the male conscience may or may not even feel a twinge of guilt about making a different choice. "Moving right along."

In the book, he shares how he was motivated in two ways to put his thoughts in writing. Firstly, by the types of calls he was being asked by women callers on his live radio talk show.

Secondly, by a "booty chaser" who was dating Harvey's daughter, with obviously less than pristine motives. Harvey strongly suggested that women set a pre-determined amount of time in mind before "giving up the cookies." (As a Christian, I believe the suitable timeframe is "after the wedding")

One key point that I took away from this book is that "self respect" needs to still be the first law of "female" survival. Without it, you can become just "raw meat." Another key point is that the woman, and her *only*, holds the key to the treasure. Value it or trash it – your choice!!

> ...there are definitely some differences between males and females – some which are innate (inherited) and some which are learned (conditioned by environment).

The interesting thing to note is that there appear to be significantly fewer books on the market written by female authors about the differences, than by male writers. So, what would motivate me to flow against the tide, and address the subject?

My incentive for taking on the subject of the female-to-male or male-to-female perspective is my interest in females coming to a better understanding of ourselves. Life is not *"just"* about hormones and cycles and kids and boyfriends and husbands and jobs and pets!! *It's about ME too!!*

Chapter 2

"How Different Are We?"

I assert that males and females are <u>not</u> *"entirely"* different, no more so than the various parts of your body are entirely different. The right arm is not the same as the left arm, and the right eye is not the same as the left eye. The left hemisphere of your brain isn't the same as the right hemisphere.

Each part is *similar* to the corresponding part; yet there are *distinctions* in each individual body part. Yet, the parts are all still part of the same body!! As male and female, we are all part of the same "body" known as "man." (Humans)

For example, each of the two hemispheres of the human brain differs in its processes, functions, perceptions, behaviors, and voluntary and involuntary responses. But, in reality, despite the differences, the two spheres are a continuum of one brain. So it is with the interface of the male and female in our realm of existence, and not just in the romantic or sexual relationship.

It is totally true that life and situations and relationships often bring about conflict or misunderstandings or disappointment or heartaches or disillusionment. However, the reality of the matter is that, as women, there is still the real potential of a "healthy balance" between us and others.

"Others" also include persons of the opposite sex – whether husband, son, father, neighbor, boyfriend or friends. To live in harmony, it is definitely necessary to have a basic understanding about relationships – me to you, you to me, us to we, and me to me.

Once, as I was preparing a message to share at a women's conference, I began to ponder the question, "How can we as women better understand 'who' we are and 'how' we are to function?" Just as importantly, can we understand why we so often 'malfunction'?

> ...is definitely helpful to have a reasonable grasp about relationships – me to you, you to me, us to we, and me to me.

In his book, "Understanding the Purpose and Power of the Woman", Dr. Myles Munroe makes two points which directly relate to our topic.[5] The first is, *"Purpose determines design"* and secondly, *"When purpose is not understood, abuse will result"*.

As we look back through recorded world history and up through to the present, we find that women have generally been considered to be not only different, but also the "lesser" among humans.

There have been a few exceptions, and in some of the more developed countries, women have had greater liberties and opportunities. However, in comparison to men, we generally still somehow end up with the short end of the stick. From a generalized view, and in almost every culture, women have been, and are still perceived as:

- Inferior to men – of lower degree or quality
- Objects for sensual gratification only – subject to sexual abuse, even by spouse

---

[5]Munroe, M. *Understanding the Purpose and Power of the Woman*. Whitaker House: Pennsylvania, 2001

- Weak, incapable of real physical strength – often victims of aggression and abuse
- Lacking in intelligence – not allowed to read or be educated
- Nothing of value to contribute to society except babies – not considered fit for public office or professional jobs outside the home
- Chattel, personal property of men – not permitted to have own bank accounts or credit
- Personal servants- whose only purpose is to meet the needs of their master – often denied medical care, required to accept other "wives"
- Domestic slaves, to be used as desired objects to be passed around until finished with and then discarded – divorced at will, often with no material or personal valuables
- Subhuman – no recognition of personal rights
- Deserving of abuse – often blamed for being the "cause"; "Look what you made me do."

I propose to you that it is time out for both women and men to misunderstand the "design" and the "purpose" for this absolutely "splendiferous" (my word) creation that God Himself "formed". This book is, in no way, intended to disparage the male creation, but the goal here is to bring healing to us females.

For thousands of years, the daughters of Eve have been looked upon through eyes distorted by more "Evil" than "Good", and have been treated as such.[6] The mindset has been that all of the world's woes are Eve's fault - because she ate the fruit first and then gave to Adam. This has been used consciously and unconsciously, to justify "abuse" of God's design.

To make matters worse, the self perception (inner eyes) of most women have been so altered by shame and guilt, that as with "glaucoma", we blindly "see" ourselves through distorted lens. Hundreds of thousands of females have believed the lie that *we are good for nothing*.

Women have been, and continue to be, misunderstood and degraded around the world, by those who refuse to receive the light of truth. The

---

[6] Genesis 3:5

result is emotional, physical, and spiritual distress and all types of inhumane abuse.

But God...

Sisters, we should just lift our hands and say, *"Hallelujah."* The wonderful thing is that God is beginning to pull the cover off of the long-standing deception. Yes, we know that Eve ate the fruit, and gave her husband with her...but the story didn't just end there. The point is...*he* ate it, and there is more to it!!

As Dr. Munroe writes, "There have been some notable examples of women throughout history who have been able to accomplish great things, display exceptional work and talent, and contribute much to society. Yet, the majority has not been allowed to develop their unique personalities and gifts fully so that they may enrich their own lives and their husbands, their families, their churches, their communities, and the world."[7]

I realize that in order for us to know how we have arrived where we are now, we would do well to take a look at the point from which we started. Therefore, it behooves us to go back to the book of beginnings, or the Biblical book of "Genesis".

---

[7] "Understanding Women, Dr. Myles Munroe, Kindle Edition, Location 177-178

"How" did we come into existence and "Why"? Answering these questions will help us to better understand "what" we do and "why" we do it.

Chapter 3

"Genetics"

Many years ago, my Pastor used to make a statement which was very thought provoking. He would say that "In every man, there is a certain amount of female, and in every woman, there is a certain amount of male." He would explain his statement by talking about various aspects of humanity, including the physicality and the emotionality.

In this chapter, I will address the physical perspective. Let's do a brief review of the "physiological" aspect of human gender by going to the field of "Human Genetics." Let's get a better understanding of sexual differentiation. To begin with, *I fully believe the Biblical account of creation.* God created the man first, and then formed the woman out of the rib which He took from Adam's side.

Realistically, for me to believe the Biblical account is one thing. However, the more important issue is whether there is scientific proof of the likelihood of the biblical account being true.

Unquestioned belief in something doesn't equal validity.

Medical and scientific evidence confirms that in the order of nature in human procreation and conception, the male is still the foundation. Conception still functions in such a way that it is through the male (sperm) that the gender of the child is determined. As research has proven, the "male" still carries within him the chromosome for both male and female, while the "woman" only carries the female chromosome.

> Every "man" still carries within him the chromosome for both male and female.

a. Review:[8]
    i. Chromosomes are threadlike molecules which carry hereditary information from height to eye color (as well as other more subtle physical qualities like how a person walks, and etc.). They are made up of protein and one molecule

---

[8] http://www.livescience.com

of DNA, which contains an organism's genetic instructions, passed down from parents. In humans, chromosomes are arranged in pairs within the nucleus of a cell. Humans have 22 of these chromosome <u>pairs</u>, called autosomes (44 in total).
ii. Humans also have an additional pair which determines gender. The sex chromosomes are referred to as X and Y, and *their combination determine a person's sex (gender)*. Females have two (XX) chromosomes while males have a pair of (XY).
iii. Whether a fetus has XX or XY chromosomes is *determined when a sperm fertilizes* a female egg (ovum). Unlike the body's other cells, the cells in the egg and in sperm (gametes or sex cells) possess *only one chromosome*.
iv. During fertilization, gametes from the sperm (male) combine with gametes from the egg (female) to form a zygote

(develops into the baby). [The zygote receives 23 chromosomes from the Dad and 23 from the Mom.]

    v. All of the gametes in the mother's eggs possess only XX chromosomes. Gametes from the father's sperm contain about half X and half Y. <u>The sperm is the variable factor (deciding) in determining the sex of the baby.</u> If the sperm which fertilizes the egg carries an X, it will combine with the X chromosome in the egg to form a female. If the sperm carries a Y, it will result in a male.

b. All humans (male and female) carry one X chromosome retained from the mother's (female) XX chromosomes.

    i. Female (XX) – have one X from the mother and the other X from the father (**which he has retained from his mother**). Since the father retains his X chromosome from his mother, a female infant has received one X chromosome from the paternal grandmother (father's side) and one X from the mother.

ii. Male (XY) – has X from the mother and Y from the father. [_Sperm cells carry **either** X or Y_]

How absolutely awesome is it that scientific evidence strongly agrees with the Biblical account. When God created Adam, the woman was created within him. Wow!!

Gen 1:27 KJV - *So God created man in his [own] image, in the image of God created he him; male and female created he them.*

Chapter 4

"'Man' at Creation"

The Biblical text in Gen 1:26 states, *"And God said, Let us make <u>man</u> in our image, after our likeness: and let <u>them</u> have dominion…the earth."*

There is a crucial point that I would like to mention here. In the above verse, we see two phases of God's creation of man. We note that God said, "Let us make <u>man</u>…" (Emphasis mine) The original Hebrew word "man" in the beginning of the verse is talking about the "image" of God, which is a spirit.

Jn 4:24 says, "God is a Spirit." Paul says in Gal. 3:28, "There is neither…male nor female: for ye are all one in Christ Jesus (our spirits). Jesus said in Jn. 3:6, "That which is born of the flesh is flesh; and that which is born of the Spirit is spirit." (Note the capital "S" is God's Spirit, small "s" is human spirit) When talking about the human spirit, the Bible doesn't differentiate between male and female. Mankind's spirit is "gender neutral", neither male nor female. I'll elaborate shortly.

In the second half of Gen. 1:26, we find the second phase of man's "triune" creation (earthy, not the divine Trinity) "...and let *them* have dominion..." Herein, we have a challenge exerted by the translation into the English language. Linguists have determined that the word "him" or "man" can be interpreted to mean "man" (male) or "mankind" (male and female), depending upon the context in which the word is used.

Within the proper context of the beginning of verse 26, the Hebrew word for "man", is correctly interpreted meaning "*spirit* of mankind (gender neutral). Following this, in verse 26, the "them" is interpreted as "mankind" (male and female, including *soul and body*). Stay with me now, this is crucial to understand!!

God spoke and created the human *spirit* (ex nihilo, from nothing that previously existed), which was, and always will be, **gender neutral.** "For Thou hast made "him" (proper translation "mankind" – BOTH male and female) a little lower than Elohim." (Psa. 8:5)

Some versions say, "Angels" but the original text translates to "Elohim". (Creator God) When speaking about Jesus, the heavenly Son of God, the writer of Heb. 1:4-5 wrote, Being so much better than the angels, as he hath by inheritance obtained a more excellent name than they. For unto which of the angels said He at any time, Thou art my Son, this day have I begotten thee? And again, I will be to him a Father, and he shall be to me a Son? " Further, in verse 7 the writer wrote, "And of the angels He saith, Who maketh His angels spirits (small "s"), and His ministers a flame of fire."

Why am I expounding on this point? Because the focus of this book is for women (and men) to see the value of ourselves according to how the One who created us sees us – not according to the damaged and distorted "world image of ourselves!!

ALL of us are the seed and lineage of Adam – and in Luke 3:38 the Bible clearly states, "…which was the son of Adam, which was the son of God." (Created in God's image and likeness) Rom 8:29 says, "For whom He did foreknow, He also did predestinate to be conformed to the image of His Son, that He might be the firstborn among many brethren" (humankind such as the earthly "man" Jesus).

ONLY "man" (mankind – male and female) was created in the image of God – not angels or any other created being. God's "image' was created as **similar** to God as any being could be, **without being God. Only** the Creator is God).

This is not a book on theology, but we are laying a premise for how we "ALL" began, and why women have equal rights, too. The <u>design</u> of all God's creations is determined by the requirements of ***His*** <u>purpose</u> for it. The "purpose" for the human spirit is to worship and have direct fellowship and communion with God.

Once the spirit of man was created "in God", God moved on to complete the second phase of man's creation. This involved the soul and body – by which "man" would not only have "direct fellowship" with God, but also have a "direct fellowship" with the physical earth realm and to one another. A physical vehicle was needed to have (1) dominion and (2) to multiply.

God "blew" the first "man" (spirit) into the lump of clay molded from the earth (body). Then God's creative power brought into existence a "never in the universe before" entity (soul) inside of that body, coexistent with the created human spirit. No other being in the universe was like that one!! Adam (male-man) was God's greatest creation!! God placed in "his" body and soul the characteristics and attributes which made him a "male".

The newly manifested entity called "soul" is believed to consist of the mind, will and emotions of "man" and is neither fully earthly nor fully heavenly. It is actually the metamorphosis of the two realms coming together. It is not currently known exactly of what "substance" (so to speak) the soul is made. However, one thing we do know for sure, every human being has one.

The brain-mind housing/connection is a finite example to "somewhat" demonstrate this mystery of creation. The brain which houses the mind can be seen and handled physically, but the thoughts in the mind come from an unseen and immaterial source (spiritual realm). Then, the effects of the thoughts are demonstrated through the physical manifestations in our bodies and environment.

Science has proven that the actual working of the male brain differs from the female brain. "The cortices of the female brain are more connected between the right and left hemispheres, which facilitates emotional processing and the ability to infer other's intentions in social interactions. (Intuitive thinking) In the male brain, the cortex is more connected front to rear, in each separate hemisphere, creating greater ability between perception and action."[9] (Rational thinking)

It's not our imagination; we are uniquely different. Yet, we are "…fearfully and wonderfully

---

[9] http://www.the-scientist.com/?articles.view/articleNo/38539/title/Male-and-Female-Brains-Wired-Differently/

made…and that my soul knoweth right well." Psa. 139:14

In order for the full plan of God on the earth to be accomplished, God created "man" as two "identical" spirits (neither male or female), and put them each in a vessel - with distinctions made in each soul and body. The *purpose and function* of the "male" or "female" *soul and body* is where the distinctions of gender are housed. Both are equal in *value, fellowship and relationship* to God, who created both with divine purpose and function.

Let me repeat that again:

The *purpose and function* of the "male" or "female" *soul and body* is where the distinctions of gender are housed. Both are equal in *value, fellowship and relationship* to God, who created both with divine purpose and function.

The *purpose and function* of the "male" or "female" *soul and body* is where the distinctions of gender are housed. Both are equal in *value, fellowship and relationship* to God, who created both with divine purpose and function.

It is most important to remember that the **designs** of God's creations are determined by the **requirements** of God's **purposes** for them. For example, the "male-man" was given more strength/focus in his body so he could till the ground as provider and protector.

On the other hand, the "female-man" was given more strength/focus in her emotions (soul) to be the loving and sensitive nurturer and helpmeet. Amazingly, women have double the number of nerve cells in certain areas of our bodies than men, making us more sensitive to pain and pleasure. (34 nerve fibers per sq. cm. compared to the male's 17 per sq. cm.)[10] I promise you; I am not making this stuff up.

In the sovereign order of creation, the "male-man" was created first. In doing this, God established that Adam is the <u>foundation</u> of all humanity. That's why the "male-man" will always be the head in the earth realm. (Ladies, no rotten tomatoes please).

This was not by coincidence, and not because Adam is "better". Remember, God's design for everything He creates is determined by its purpose. Both creations of "man" (male and female) are <u>equal</u> in essence, but each has a <u>different</u> purpose and order!! (Hold the tomatoes please)

While Adam was alone in the garden, God taught him to interact with God, and how to interact with the earth. God showed Adam his purpose and functions including being the leader, the teacher, the cultivator, the provider and the

---

[10] http://m.livescience.com/7527-5-painful-facts.html

protector. Then it was time for the completion of "man's" creation.

(Drum roll please) Then, God took the rib of Adam, "formed" it into the female body, and went through the same process as He did with Adam. He blew the created spirit (God's spirit/breath) into the form/body. Then He created in her the soul (mind, will, emotions) with female characteristics to accommodate her female form. This was now the "female-man", Eve.

By the time Eve was brought onto the scene, God and the male-man had prepared the physical environment for her. Her "spirit" had been created of God, and was of exactly the same nature as Adam's "spirit." They each had the identical ability to worship and commune directly with God. Adam was the "head" in the earth; and God was (and still is) the "head" over all.

This is so important for us to understand that I will repeat it again. Eve's "spirit man" was created of God, and was of exactly the same nature as Adam's "spirit man"; with the exact identical ability to worship and commune directly with God. Adam was the "head" in the earth, and God was (and still is) the "head" over all.

Eve's spirit was of the same created essence as Adam's, and her body was birthed from Adam's body. However, her "soul" (consisting of mind, will, and emotions) was uniquely different. That's why the "two had to become one." They had to be introduced to each other, and they had to meld together, just like every husband and wife since them. Her unique design was determined <u>by the purpose</u> God had for her.

"For You created my inmost being (*spirit*); you knit me (*soul*) together in my mother's womb. I praise You because I am fearfully and wonderfully made. Your works are wonderful, I know that right well. My *frame* was not hidden from You, when I was in the secret place, when I was *woven together* in the depths of the earth (mother's body), Your eyes saw my *unformed body*; all the days ordained for me were written in Your book *before one of them came to be*." Psa 139:13-16 (*Emphasis mine*)

My God, my God, my God…

Chapter 5

"Male at Creation"

In Gen 1:27, let's give close attention to the words, "So God <u>*created man*</u> in His own image, in the image of God created <u>*he him*</u>; male and female <u>*created he them*</u>.

Here, again, we have a challenge created by the insertion of punctuation when the text was translated into English, and how we use the sometimes confusing English language. Here conjoined into one sentence, we actually have *2 separate* events that occurred at *2 different points* of time. The difference in time could have been a split second, and is unknown to us.

Chapter 1:26-28 is not a detailed description, but rather a birds' eye view of the process, which is later repeated and explained in timely detail in Gen 2:15-23.

How do we know this to be true? Genesis 2:8, 15-20 very clearly demonstrates that there was a period of time (during the 6th "day" of creation) when Adam was in the garden *alone* completing his major tasks. While he was learning to "rule" over his domain, and receiving instructions from God, "Eve" was not visible on the scene yet.

Also, please notice that during that time, the only major task/commandment which God had not yet given to Adam was to "be fruitful and multiply". What is unknown is how long a "creation day" lasted, in terms of time as we understand it. Was it 24 hours, 1,000 years, or some other time span? (2 Pet. 3:8) We don't know.

> ...that there was a period of time (during the 6th "day" of creation) when Adam was in the garden *alone*...

Gen 2:15–19 "And the LORD God took the man, and put him into the Garden of Eden to dress it and to keep it. And the LORD God commanded the man, saying, Of every tree of the garden thou mayest freely eat: But of the tree of the knowledge of good and evil, thou shalt not eat of it: for in the day that thou eatest thereof thou shalt surely die.

And the LORD God said, it is not good that the man should be alone; I will make him an help meet for him. And out of the ground the LORD God formed every beast of the field, and every fowl of the air; and brought them unto Adam to see what he would call them: and whatsoever Adam called every living creature, that was the name thereof. And Adam gave names to all cattle, and to the fowl of the air, and to every beast of the field; <u>but for Adam there was not found an help meet for him</u>.

It is very important for us to notice that prior to this point in time, Adam was the only "man" (human) physically visible and operating in the garden. The "dominion" over the earth was given to, and exercised by Adam *alone,* including the dressing/keeping of the garden and the naming of the animals.

This is not a book primarily about men, so I won't go further here. Look for my upcoming book on this topic.

Chapter 6

"Female at Creation"

Let's take another look at Genesis 1:27-28. I ask you to notice that the Bible does not say, "In the image of God created He him *and* then created He her." Rather, the text says, "...created He *him (mankind)*; male and female created Him *them*." Out of "one" creation came male and female. That's the "spirit" of human (male and female) which was created <u>*in*</u> God before God ever placed in into houses of clay.

Genesis 1:28 says, "And God blessed <u>them</u>, and God said to <u>them</u>, be fruitful and multiply" This is another crucial point of information for us as we look at what was going on *before* woman was brought "out" onto the scene.

Remember this, "The woman was made <u>by</u> the will of God for the man," not vice versa. Equally important is the fact that the woman was made to be protected and provided for by the man, not vice versa. (No rocks, please)

Let us take a look, again at modern scientific evidence that supports the validity of the Biblical account of what took place when God took the rib from Adam.

Gen 2:21-23 *"And the Lord God caused a deep sleep to fall upon Adam, and he slept: and He took one of his ribs, and closed up the flesh instead thereof; And the rib, which the Lord God had taken from man, made He a woman...taken out of man."*

    a. "Birthed" out of Adam, directly from the rib (genetic) tissue of his body – formed into the woman (taken out of, but yet a part of)
        1) Help Meet – to provide "like" love, affection and relationship. Adam was "alone" until one "like" him was prepared.
        2) Mother of his children
    b. The "Rib"
    Dr. Georgia Purdom[11] states "All bones can repair themselves but only ribs can regenerate themselves." In

---

[11]http//:wwwanswersingenesis.org/articles – Dr. Georgia Purdom, AIG-US on February 4, 2009: "The Amazing Regenerating Rib"

"Clinically Oriented Anatomy", we find:[12]

1) Ribs are commonly removed and used during surgeries that require bone grafts in other parts of the body. The rib is removed from the periosteum (a tissue surrounding the bone) much like a banana would be removed from its peel while keeping the peel intact). The periosteum <u>must</u> remain intact, as it contains osteoblasts (specialized cells) which build the new rib bone.
2) Functions of the rib: (1) Protection for the lungs and heart; form a "cage" (2) One of few bones that continue to make red marrow (thus blood cells) in the adult. (3) They are attachment points for the chest muscles involved in respiration (inhalation and exhalation);

---

[12] [Keith L. Moore and Arthur F. Dailey, "Clinically Oriented Anatomy, 4th ed. (Philadelphia: Lippincott Williams & Wilkins, 1999) p.64]

whereby the very breath of life needed for each body cell is transported. (Another physiological form of "help meeting - helping to carry life") *Whoo Hoo! You go girl!!*

> take a look, again physiologically, at modern scientific evidence that supports the validity of the Biblical account of what took place when God took the rib from Adam.

Gen 2:21-23 reveals a never changing principal which was established by God from the very beginning. If we are not careful, our environment will cause us to overlook the depth of this truth. Just remember that Eve (the rib) was <u>not created separately</u> from Adam but, in fact, was taken "out of" Adam.

When God formed Adam, the "rib" from which He would later "form" the woman was inside Adam's body, fully covered. She was a part of his actual physical person. The woman was never "alone". Her entire existence and purpose was within the realm of "in relationship" – first in

God, and then in Adam. "Woman never existed as a creation "alone". I cannot stress that too much.

Now, wait a minute or two, don't get your knickers in a knot again. Stay with me! I'm going somewhere, and when we get there, you'll be happy you didn't throw the book away.

Notice in Gen 2:18, when God first made the statement, "It is not good that the man should be *alone*..." it was not Adam who asked for a help *"meet"* for himself, but it was God who made the decision. *Up to this point*, Adam was working so hard, he probably didn't notice that something was missing. He didn't ask God for it. If you have never tasted sugar, you don't know what "sweet" is – or what you're missing. *Oh my!!!!!!*

Someone may say, "Why is it significant that Adam did not recognize the need?" or "What difference does it make?" I propose to you that on **this seemingly insignificant issue, hinges much of the confusion and ambiguity about the roles of males and females.** This includes socially, mentally, emotionally and in the way we "see" our world.

> Her entire existence and purpose was to be within the realm of "in relationship". "Woman never existed as a creation "alone".

The fact of the matter is that from the very beginning, the woman's *perspective was different* from the man's. This was not a *result* of the "Fall" – but rather, was by the "Order of Creation". Only God could take "1" creation, turn it into "2" beings with distinct characteristics, and then make them together a complete uniquely combined "1"!

Later, as a result of the "Fall" – there was introduced into the disposition of the woman two characteristics that were not a part of God's original design for her. Along with her new knowledge of good "and" evil, the seeds were planted for the traits of "individualism" and "independence". I'll deal with this in detail in a later chapter.

Chapter 7

"Are Men and Women 'Incompatible'?"

How did the chasm that seems so uncrossable at times between men and women come to be? In fairness to all, I would like to take a look again at the Book of Beginnings to see if there is a valid reason for these "differences".

Because each one of the pieces of a 500-piece jigsaw puzzle is different in shape and/or color, are they not really pieces cut from the same puzzle? Or is this a bunch of malarkey that men just make up to keep from dealing with women, children, and issues in the home when they're tired (unlike women who just keep going, tired and all).

Perhaps a future book could be, "Adam's Eyes". Of course, I would need an Adam to co-author it with me, to see in "Man-ganese"?

Before Eve was ever formed from Adam's rib and brought onto the scene in Eden, everything in the environment was set up and prepared for her. Everything was set in place to make her flourish and be a happy, healthy, and loving person - physically, emotionally, and spiritually complete. She was "covered", cared for by her man, and in complete fellowship with God.

Her nature and origin was never to be on her own, or the provider or a single parent or head of the household. Hold on to that thought and don't start hyperventilating!!!! Ladies and gents, I need for you to put a safety pin in your knickers right at this point, truly park your mind and focus for a bit, and reeeeally pay close attention. This is a pivotal point about the issue of "differences".

> ...is this a bunch of malarkey that men just make up to keep from dealing with women, children and issues...

In the beginning Eve was the apple of the man's eye, in every sense of the word – bone of his bone, flesh of his flesh. (Gen. 2:23) That may be a challenging concept for us to grasp in our present imaginations because of our Western culture of **"individualism"** and **"independence"**.

It is a fact that in light of God's introduction (revelation) of the "rib" to the one from which she was taken, Adam was able to declare without question that man should, "...*cleave* unto his wife; and they shall be one flesh." (Gen. 2:24). (Emphasis mine)

As we take a closer look at the word "cleave" in Webster's dictionary, we find two forms of the word "cleave" – the "intransitive" verb and the "transitive" verb. The significance of the word has to be understood within the context that it is used at a particular place and time.[13]

The "intransitive" verb form of "cleave" means "**To adhere firmly and closely or loyally and unwaveringly**." This type of verb has two characteristics. First, it is an "action verb", expressing a do-able activity (i.e. Go, sit, arrive). Second, it will not have a direct object receiving the action".

The "intransitive" verb form of "cleave" means "To adhere firmly and closely or loyally and unwaveringly."

---

[13] http://www.meriamwebsterdictionary.com

[Before The Fall]

In other words, in the beginning, prior to the "Fall", the "cleaving" that Adam did "unto" Eve, was the "do-able activity" (his purposeful action) of "adhering firmly and closely, loyally and unwaveringly" to her. There was <u>no other person, thought or focus</u> in between them. They were as one; in complete unity (NO individualism or independence).

> If you don't get anything else out of this book, please don't miss this!

[Fall ->-> knowledge of good + evil ->-> shame, guilt]

[After the Fall]

However, the transitive verb form of "cleave" means "To **divide** by or as if by a **cutting** blow. To **separate** into **distinct parts** and especially into groups having **divergent views**."

Honestly, I didn't make this stuff up!!

Let's dig a little deeper. Webster further defines "transitive" as "Being characterized by having or containing a direct object. Being or relating to a relation with the property that if the relation holds between a first element and a second element and between the second element and a third, it holds between the first and third elements.

In other words, Adam "divided by a cutting blow" (with his words) and "separated into distinct parts" his *relationship* (oneness) from Eve (himself from her) - when he pronounced to God, "the woman whom thou gavest to be with me..." (Gen. 3:12)

My interpretation of what the brother said is this -"God, she is not really MY woman or a part of me anymore. Whatever happens now is between you and her. Don't include me."

The transitive verb form of "cleave" means "To **divide** by or as if by a **cutting** blow. To **separate** into **distinct parts** and especially into groups having **divergent views**."

If you look back at the last part of the transitive verb definition, you will see *"...into groups having divergent views."* Once Eve was "thrust off" by Adam, in an instant, she <u>learned</u> to begin to stand and think as an <u>individual, independently</u> from her husband.

Her explanation did not involve him – she didn't say, "The serpent beguiled me and I shared it with Adam." Rather, she said, "...and I did eat." I believe she realized she was on her own.

"Transitive" – characterized by having or containing a direct object. Previously there was no "object" (anything or anyone) separating Adam and Eve, they were "one" and totally compatible physically, mentally, emotionally, and spiritually.

But, after the Fall, they now had a "direct object" standing <u>between</u> them [shame and guilt]. This could not unite them, but rather caused a division between them. They now had separate concerns, separate ideologies, separate focuses, and individual shame and guilt.

The "divergent views" showed up immediately in the very next generation, in the two sons who were nothing alike in their dispositions. I am definitely not trying to justify one and accuse the other. Rather, I am in hot pursuit to help us as women to "see" more clearly how we have come to view ourselves a certain way.

Perhaps the mindset which our individualistic and independent culture perpetuates, may be adding to some of our worse nightmares, rather than helping us to build relationships and lives we so longingly dream of.

Definitions:[14]

Individualism – (1) a doctrine that the interests of the individual are or ought to be paramount; also; conduct guided by such a doctrine. (2); the perception that all values, rights, and duties originate in individuals.

Independent – (1) not dependent: not subject to control by others (self governing); not affiliated with a larger controlling unit. (2) not looking to others for one's opinions or for guidance in conduct. (3) not requiring or relying on others (as for care or livelihood. (4): not determined by or capable of being deduced or derived from or expressed in terms of members of the set under consideration (ex. *Family, community, church*)

---

[14]http://www.merriamwebsterdictionary.com

I would like to insert a tone of caution here as myriads of us are striving to insist on having our individual "rights", and as we assert our ever-increasing roles as "an independent" woman. Are we allowing wisdom to help guide us so that the disintegration of our families and other relationships are not the "at any cost" factor? I'm just saying…

Let's not get it twisted!! I am not suggesting that women should be clingy, whiny, begging, super needy, neurotic and unable to do anything on our own. ("I've got to have a man – any man, no matter what.").

Neither do I support the completely opposite mindset which some women have developed, especially many in business or a profession, or many of the younger generation. ("I don't need a man for nothing (but sex) because I have my own job/business, car and house; and I can take care of my own self and my kids.")

And, while I'm here, let me say that I am definitely ***not*** a proponent for the formal "Women's Lib Movement." As far as I'm concerned, the "male-man" is the best thing since the world began, and there is no substitute. Sadly, hindsight has shown that there were some ulterior motives promulgated by the Women's Liberation

Movement that were not in true favor for women. Period.

Yes, I still love to have doors opened for me, the heavy things carried for me, my dinner at the restaurant paid for, the kids disciplined for me, and etc., without feeling like I'm a traitor to my sister-girls. Even if we work in a leadership position, I believe it should be done graciously; and when it's time to go home, I need to be protected, provided for and treated like a lady.

I know it's a moot point, but I'll say it anyway. I wish the amount of money, time and energy that has been exerted to put forth a mindset and lifestyle that has helped with the disintegration of the traditional family, would have been better spent providing education, jobs and skills for females and males of all ages, who are struggling to survive and provide for their families in our recession riddled society.

We need to get busy developing and building on skills to live in healthy relationships with ourselves, our men and our children. There's no need for a "Women's Lib Rebellion." How about a "Liberated Woman's Movement?" (Power to the People!!) Oops! Back to reality.

In the beginning, Eve was in complete oneness with the man – two halves of the same whole. Then, doing what she thought was right at the time; she shared her goodies with her man, "from her heart".

The next thing she knew, she and every female after her was considered "damaged goods." Since then, the greatest challenges of women at large have been how to deal with being left naked, uncovered, accused, and abused. Now that right there is a book by itself!!

The wonderful thing is that there are a lot of valuable resources available which can help us to develop a "healthy" mindset about ourselves and other women. We can begin to "see" ourselves as the precious and wonderful creations which God has made us to be. We've got to teach our young ones coming up.

Woman – yes, you are awesomely created!!

Chapter 8

"Help Meet or Floor Mat?"

One thing that is extreeeeemely important for us to remember is that there was a _delay in time_ between when God placed the male in the Garden, and the time that God took the rib out of the man from which He "made" the female (Gen. 2:22).

Therefore, at man's beginning and for an unknown amount of time afterwards, he was alone. He did not have to interact with, talk to, show affection or be responsible for the care of another human.

Did you ever wonder why God had to "command" Adam with instructions for him to "forsake all others and cleave only to his wife?" This seems odd since there were no other people around at that time. Duh!!

> Gen 2:18 KJV - And the LORD God said, [It is] not good that the man

should be alone; I will make him an "help", meet for him.

One of the major challenges for us, again, is how the English language tends to be so fluid that it allows us to manipulate a word to make it "fit" or "meet" what we "want it" to say. This can be confusing. This portion of scripture is one of the most misquoted and misrepresented scriptures in the Bible. Even I myself am guilty of running the two words "help meet" together.

However, I pray that the Spirit of truth and revelation causes our light bulbs to come on. (Eph 1:17-18) We need a better grasp on just *who* we are and *what* we are to be doing, as women. Let me just read the same scripture from several different versions:

> Gen 2:18 KJV - And the LORD God said, [It is] not good that the man should be alone; I will make him a help, *meet* for him.

> Gen 2:18 NLT - Then the LORD God said, "It is not good for the man to be alone. I will make a helper who is *just right* for him."

Gen 2:18 NIV - The LORD God said, "It is not good for the man to be alone. I will make a helper *suitable for* him."

Gen 2:18 RSV - Then the LORD God said, "It is not good that the man should be alone; I will make him a helper *fit for* him."

Gen 2:18 AMP - Now the Lord God said, It is not good (sufficient, satisfactory) that the man should be alone; I will make him a helper *meet (suitable, adapted, complementary) for* him.

Gen 2:18 NKJV - And the LORD God said, "[It is] not good that man should be alone; I will make him a helper *comparable to* him." Comparable = similar, resembling, matching. (This version has changed the preposition from "for" to "to", which can be (and often is) taken Biblically out of context to give an illusion of a sense of competition. Not the original context of the scripture.

Profound Statement #1 – <u>What</u> is the **purpose** for which **God** made us? - The woman was made **for** the man, not the man for the woman. The man was made **for** God.

We are to "help" - not "make", manipulate, coddle, persuade or seduce him into doing what's right. What are we to "Help" him to do? <u>"Help" the man to accomplish what God has called him to do.</u> This includes respecting and loving him, bearing and nurturing his children, and setting the atmosphere of the home. Each man has a purpose for which God has called him – and every, every, every single one of them need "help" from a female – whether wife, mother, sister, friend, and etc. Not "help" by being the "voice of God" in his ears or in the lives of our children. I just need to park right here for a bit. (No rotten eggs, please!!)

There is a very crucial point of human history that the enemy of our soul tries to make us rush to judgment on. He continues to use this to create havoc in the relationships of males to females, and females to males.

According to what the word of God says, the rib from which **God** "made" the woman was taken by **God** from where - from the man.

Now, please don't get your knickers all in kinks about what I am getting ready to say. I am going to read 3 verses and then make some important points.

> *Gen 2:21 KJV - And the LORD God caused a deep sleep to fall upon Adam, and he slept: and he took one of his ribs, and closed up the flesh instead thereof;*
>
> *Gen 2:22 KJV - And the rib, which the LORD God had taken from man, made he a woman, and brought her unto the man. [Read 3x]*
>
> *Gen 2:23 KJV - And Adam said, This [is] now bone of my bones, and flesh of my flesh: she shall be called Woman, because she was taken out of Man.*

Again, a crucial point that we MUST remember, always is that the Woman **was never created separately** from the man. She was initially created within the man. Even when God pulled her out and "made" her into her own form, she was still an extension/connected to the male-man.

That's why Adam made the profound statement, "This is now bone of my bone, and flesh of my flesh." In this context, this "Bone" is physical, but this "Flesh" is above and beyond the physical body. What a pure Rhema (divinely inspired) revelation revealed to Him by God Himself.

For example, it's easy enough for most adults to clearly "see" that because of human anatomy, during the act of sexual intercourse, the male is the donor, and the female is the receiver. However, what is less clearly understood by many of us is the "more important" truth – that the giving and receiving is not just "physical". The interaction also impacts the spirit and the soul (mind, will and emotion).

The reason for this is because that is how we were created and formed from the beginning – to fulfill the purpose and design of God, the creator. God intended it to be so!! That's what makes a true marriage!!

An electric cord can lie on the floor next to a receptacle forever, without accomplishing one single thing. However, when the two are connected, power is available to bring forth dynamic life!!

Hold on to your pantyhose right here!!! We were NEVER created to be independent and without a covering of a male, <u>ever</u> at any time in our <u>earthly lives</u> – not as children or adults!! Say what…………..???????????

<u>That</u> is why God had to command the woman that her desire was to be ***"unto"*** her husband, and that he shall rule over her. Not as a curse, but for her protection and provision, even after the Fall!!!!!!!!***Not as a curse***, but for her protection and provision!!!!!!!

And one more time - **Not as a curse**, but for her protection and provision!!!!!!!

God had to give her instructions just as he had to give Adam instructions. This part of God's statement to Eve was ***not a judgment***, or a curse, as some have taught. That was God's instruction to the woman of ***how to be reconciled to her husband.*** After all, there was still purpose to be fulfilled.

Of course, the enemy of our souls has twisted the meaning of God's words. However, we see the same position of the woman taught in the New Testament by the Apostle Paul, speaking to women who have been reconciled to God by grace through Jesus Christ. How can it be a part of a curse?

For the woman's "desire" to be unto her husband is *not* now, and never was meant to be, a curse. When we put our finest china "under" the protection of the china closet instead of in the banged-up kitchen cabinet, are we punishing the china? When you "cover" your diamonds in a safe for protection, are you punishing the diamonds?

Let's take a look at the insidious message that has been passed down from generation to generation about the "curse" which took place in the Garden of Eden. Somehow, throughout history in most cultures, females have been harshly subjugated by the subliminal message that she was "cursed" by God to be trod under by the feet of the male, while the male only got charged with working hard.

The result has been an almost universal perception of women that we are "less than," with an occasional liberated woman here and there. But is that what God intended? Not hardly.

At the point at which Adam ate the fruit which Eve did offer him, the "Word" which God had spoken to <u>**ADAM**</u> was *activated* against ***both*** of them *together*, with immediate spiritual death and eventual physical death. (Gen. 2:16-17) This was the penalty of doing what God had instructed them not to do. This was not a "curse"; this was the sequential consequence of their action; just like "A" follows "B".

It is very important to notice that God did not pronounce a "curse" on either Adam or Eve in these verses!! (Just hold on to your wig). There are only two verses where God declared a "curse:" in Gen 3:14 (serpent) and in Gen 3:17 (the ground).

Well now, you may ask, "What about Eve's monthly "curse" and being "Lord-ed over" by her husband? Isn't that proof she deserves to be treated lower than an ant hill? Certainly not!!

Yes! Their joint act of disobedience certainly did cause God to declare a penalty, in much the same way that our children's disobedience causes us to discipline them. The goal of discipline is to teach the principle of "cause and effect." God's love for Adam and Eve didn't turn to hate because they sinned, but they now had to learn that the "knowledge of good and evil" has a profound effect, with subsequent consequences. Sad to say, the effects of "sin" has been increasing ever since in their progeny, like a snowball barreling down a ski slope.

The actual "penalty" pronounced on Eve was ***exactly the same*** as it was for Adam, no more and no less. It was ***pain and "hard labor"***. After all – he and she were one!!? Why wouldn't they get the same consequence? (1) Adam would have to "toil" to bring forth fruit from the ground by the sweat of his brow - in pain (hard labor); and (2) Eve would have to toil to bring forth fruit (children) from the ground of her body by the sweat of her brow - also in pain (hard labor).

This is so simple to understand, yet it is profound. Let me repeat it again for those of us a little slower to understand than others:

The actual "penalty" pronounced on Eve was exactly the same as it was for Adam, no more and no less. It was ***pain and "hard labor"***. After all – he and she were one!!? Why wouldn't they get the same consequence? (1) Adam would have to "toil" to bring forth fruit from the ground by the sweat of his brow - in pain (hard labor); and (2) Eve would have to toil to bring forth fruit (children) from the ground of her body by the sweat of her brow - also in pain (hard labor).

Shut your mouth!! I know it was not flesh and blood that revealed that to me!! I just want to lay down on the floor right here and kick and scream for how this scripture has been taken soooo out of context for so long. For all the years of bitter oppression, and how it has been used as a whip over the head of women, instead of the provision of God's love it was meant to be; I decree that we forgive every tormentor!!

It was not without good reason that Paul warned that a man had better treat his wife right, that his prayers be not hindered. Women belong to God too. (I Pet 3:7)

Again, as per Dr. Munroe that *"When purpose is not understood, abuse will result."*[15] Eve misunderstood the "purpose" of one power which God had given her to "help" Adam. It was the "Power of Influence", and she abused it. She used it in an illegal manner, howbeit, not purposely vindictive.

Eve was deceived by the serpent just long enough for her emotions (desire) to be drawn away from Adam and redirected to the forbidden fruit.

> "And when the woman saw that the tree was good (emotional response) for food, and that it was pleasant (emotional response) to the eyes and a tree to be desired (emotional

---

[15] Understanding the Woman" Dr. Myles Munroe, Kindle Edition

response)…she took of the fruit thereof, and did eat…" (Gen 3:6)

God's intended objects for Eve's emotions were to be God Himself (Love, spiritual communion); her husband (Love, passion, desire); and their offspring (Love, nurture). God equipped Eve with the tremendous power of "female influence" so that when the times were right, she would be able to "woo" Adam away from his "task oriented/work focused" mindset towards home, wife, and family.

[**Sidebar**: Such is the disposition of men in general, even until the present time – without a woman's nudging, he might never know when to stop working; until hunger for food, and/or sex drags him down to the ground. Left on their own, they would not come home for days, or until they're about to pass out from exhaustion.]

Eve's "desire" being unto her husband did not "begin" after the "Fall"- it was one of the characteristics in her nature from the very moment that God "separated" her physically from the body of her husband. It's in the "genetic memory" of women. That's why women always have a desire (sense of longing) to be with the man they love. (Remember Bishop David Evan's book mentioned in an earlier chapter). It was all a part of God's original intention!!

[**Sidebar**: This is one of the primary reasons why a woman will stay in a prolonged relationship with an abusive man!! It's still "desire unto", albeit warped.]

Eve wasn't created to do anything on her own, without including her husband. It goes to follow that when she ate the fruit and it was good, her very first thought was to use her influence to woo Adam into sharing her newfound "pleasure" with her. All of her emotions in Gen 3:6 were "sensual" (pleasurable to the body, including eyes and mouth) – and who else would she "desire" to share her sensuality with except the only one with whom she has known sensuality to the nth degree.

Remember! All of this took place even before God came to talk to them after the Fall. In other words, the Fall absolutely did ***not*** change God's original purpose and plan for the woman. When the deceiver saw that God did not destroy Adam and Eve on the spot, he knew that he had to come up with another plan to try to "divide and conquer."

After hearing God's promise to use the woman in Gen 3:15, the deceiver set out to destroy one of the woman's greatest gifts that she could use to "help" her husband – her ability to influence him. Left to her own emotions and "intuition", without the stability of guidance from, and unity with her husband, she was like a loose cannon.

From that point forward, the enemy has had varying degrees of success in driving a wedge of distrust and contention between men and women, and in creating a sense of competitiveness to bring greater devastation.

Yes, Eve acted independently from Adam, and the results were pivotal in the greatest shipwreck of all times. But Adam ate the fruit too, and God still loved them both just as much. As the loving Creator that He is, His first directive to Eve was, "Stay under your husband where you can be protected and provided for.

However, because of the knowledge of good and evil, I believe Adam and his male children after him lost their ability to "see" and still love the woman spontaneously. In fact, it's almost as if anger and resentment began in Adam, and passed down by genetic memory to every male child. No wonder the New Testament commands the husband to "love your wife." On the other hand, the sense of shame and guilt is more pronounced in women everywhere, more so than anger.

In essence God said to Eve, "Woman, man threw you under the bus because he illegally surrendered his place of responsibility **for** you – **to** you. However, I still see you in the way in which you were created - in relationship to the man. He is still responsible for you. You are not responsible <u>for</u> him. You are responsible to me to still be a help meet for him."

How do I know this part of God's statement was not a judgment as a result of a curse? Paul, under the inspiration of the Holy Ghost, reiterated the proper relationship of Godly men and women in the Body of Christ. Actually, I believe that the reason it needed to be (still needs to be) reinforced is because of the mistreatment that women have received.

Why would he tell you to live under a curse? To "submit" or "subject to" means to 'come under' as a part of, not as a door mat, but as one <u>who relies on, trusts in, and believes in</u> the one under whom they stand. Somebody say, "Eve, where art thou?" (See Col. 3:18-19, and Eph. 5)

> *Eph 5:33 KJV - Nevertheless let every one of you in particular so love his wife even as himself; and the wife [see] that she reverence [her] husband.*

(1) The second crucial point that we MUST understand is that we were made from a portion of the anatomy of man which has the physical function of ***helping*** [somebody say "helping"]. We are <u>not</u> the *source* of life, but God causes us to be the *nurturers* of life, for men and children.

Profound statement #2 –<u>How</u> the Creator made us is simple, yet complex. He made us from the bone of the man, but added the feminine traits of unrelenting tenacity, strength, and nature of the nurturer and protector of life. (Gen. 3:12, 16)

Chapter 9

"Who Is She, Anyway'?"

"Purpose determines design." "When purpose is not understood, abuse will result."… Dr. Myles Munroe

As I think about the traditional history that is taught in schools and by society in general, I realize that the term is often misconstrued. The term "his", in this context should be like the term "man" – actually meaning "mankind, male and female". There is no story for him without her.

Things are much better than they used to be, but the chronicling of the women who have been right there alongside their men throughout the same major world events, is not as readily taught or acknowledged. Young women, who are looking for positive role models, may have to dig a little deeper than a contemporary magazine or social media.

We, as females were awesomely designed by our Creator, to be, in the words of First Lady Eleanor Roosevelt, "the 'neck' upon which the head turns." To remind us just how wonderfully gifted and endowed we all are, I'll share a much-abbreviated list of a few women who have had much impact as wives, mothers, sisters, and etc., in the making of our world's "herstory". (Just kidding)

Look at the effect that some First Ladies, the wives of our Presidents of the United States, have had in terms of social impact. These include Michelle Obama who challenged the national food industry and schools regarding the welfare of our children.

How about Nancy Reagan, who stepped aside from her successful acting career, to champion her husband? She was given credit for elevating the social life of the White House, but it was her husband who was given credit which belonged to her for initiating the "Just Say No To Drugs" campaign.

How about Jackie Kennedy who broke through the fashion ceiling for women in many walks of life? How many people know that she was also a celebrated book editor, for more than one national publishing house?

How about the powerful Eleanor Roosevelt, who was married to a man who developed polio at a time when many didn't survive. Yet, she stepped down from her world travels and her own dreams and visions to nurse him, and to help him regain his desire to live. With his wife's help, and much recognized wisdom, her husband went on to be elected President 4 times. Would he have been successful without such a strong woman? Only God knows for sure, but I think not!!

There were wives and mistresses of many other government officials, in addition to these ladies, whose husbands went home to them at night and "counseled" in the comfort of their arms, at the end of some very challenging days. I wonder how many decisions were really made by the man, alone.

How about our beloved Winnie Mandela, who "stood by her man" through the thick and the thin, and never allowed the world to forget about him while he was in prison. I had to search deep in my heart to forgive him when he "threw her under the bus" following his release. Yes, there were allegations made against her – but he was a "criminal" whom she never gave up on. *"Her desire was unto her husband."*

How about the "possibly unmarried" Oprah Winfrey, who turned the entire television industry on its ear, and has had impact in many activities with social agendas. She has never failed to reach back or to "pay it forward", including her academy for girls in South Africa. I say, 'possibly' because I believe she and Stedman are secretly married. Shhh!

How about soft-spoken Rosa Parks, wife of a little-known activist named Raymond. Her husband and other men (most notably Martin Luther King, Jr.) had been trying to build up the Civil Rights Movement for a while. Then one day, Raymond's wife said, "No, I'm too tired to stand up." Within 24 hours, the movement was thrust full steam ahead.

How about Coretta Scott King, who gave up her dreams as a celebrated concert singer and violinist, to walk side by side with her husband in the Civil Rights Movement until his assassination in 1968? She outlived him and continued with his vision for 40 years. Do we celebrate her birthday?

How about Betty Shabazz (Mrs. Malcolm X) who set aside her profession as a Registered Nurse to walk beside her husband. How many nights did these husbands share counsel with their women of wisdom?

Going back further, there was Alexander Graham Bell who (reportedly) invented the telephone. I wonder how many nights his wife, Mabel, sat up with him. How often did she comfort him when he was frustrated? Her deafness is said to have been his inspiration for the telephone, along with his mother who was also deaf.

How about Thomas Jefferson's (unmarried) wife of color, who inspired him to support and fight on the behalf of the Emancipation Proclamation?

On the negative side, it's said that Adolf Hitler's mother was a devout Catholic. However, she didn't stop her husband from being abusive to their young son. Could that have been a large part of what turned the heart of the young Adolph who was a choir boy; and who once wanted to become a priest, into a monster who hated God?

Let's look at a few examples in the Bible. People often speak about David who killed the giant, Goliath. Did you ever notice that although David was offended by the giant challenging the armies of Israel; David did not confront him until Saul offered his daughter? There's God using the "help meet" again. (I Sam. 17)

A woman was called on again to help save a kingdom, as David the king was resting in the comfort of his "nurse" Abishag, preparing to die -

while his son Adonijah was busily trying to steal the throne. God had the prophet to send Bathsheba, the "help meet" in there to get things straight before the King died. (I Kg 1)

How about Miriam, Moses' sister, whose name is chronicled in Mic. 6:4 as one of the leaders sent before the Israelites coming out of Egypt. How would you like to help lead over a half million people – all of those women with PMS and howling babies? Only another woman…

Let's bring it home - how about the millions of women, all around the world, who woke up husbands (or not) and kids this morning, and found socks for them, and fixed breakfast and sent them on their way – or who gave up their breakfast so the family would have enough.

My point is this, God designed "man" (male and female) to work together in unity to accomplish the greater purpose and good. There are no big "I"s and little "U"s really, just a different design and purpose. I guarantee you for every accomplishment of any significance, that any of us achieve, it will be because somebody, somewhere has sown into us – both male and female.

Women, ladies, la femmes, chicks, sisters, daughters, Moms, Gramms – take your rightful place. You can do it! You are awesome! If you need help, reach out – but don't give up on your dreams, plans, and destiny. Who knows? That very man that you have been called to walk beside may be a "world changer", at the very least, in the lives of his family and the place where God has called him.

…Get to steppin'

CHAPTER 10

"Intuition and Influence"

As a woman (womb-ed man, or man with a womb), there are some characteristics which God put in the nature of Eve, which are present in all females. They should be considered as tools given to empower her as a help meet. They were to enable her to function according to God's specific assignments to women.

In this chapter, I'll take a cursory look at two key female tools - intuition and influence. Remember that in the beginning, God said that everything about Eve was "very good", which included her intuition and influence.

However, when her "eyes" were opened to be able to see both "good and evil", these tools took on the potential to be used for both good and evil. These are "innate" traits within every female, and they have a spiritual component.

It's not a question of "whether" a female has these abilities, it's merely a question of how quickly we learn and choose to use them. For example, in most cultures, it's generally accepted that women tend to have some kind of "sixth sense" (intuition) about the safety or danger of their children, even outside of their presence. Excuse me for using a New Age term, but I'm trying to make a point.

In some circles, a more acceptable term may be "discernment". (Not the same as in I Cor. 12, but as in present at physical birth.) Since this is not a book on spiritual gifts, I won't belabor this point, other than to use the example that some people are born with a gift to draw, and never have to "learn" how to. For others, like me, we draw stick people. However, I was definitely born with the "gift of gab". (And everybody say…)

One of the ways that intuition works with women is through our sensitivity to emotions. We are able to have a "sense" about things that are positive, as well as negative. For example, we can "know in our gut" when we have an uneasiness about a particular person, and your husband may think you're crazy when you try to explain it to him. Or you may be riding in the car while your husband is driving, and suddenly you'll have a "sense" for him to slow down even though he doesn't see anything in the road.

My suggestion to you is to just "help", not enforce. Tell him what you "feel", and don't get upset when he doesn't "get" what you're talking about. His rational mind is waiting to "see" it with his eyes, or "hear" it with his ears, but your God-given gift is at work to "help".

After enough close calls, he'll learn to respect and trust your "intuition". He'll avoid the guy stealing from him; or put his foot on the brakes before he runs over the small child running out between two parked cars. Just as we've learned by our experiences how to trust that inner sense, our men and children have to learn that they can trust it also.

The exact nature of intuition is a subject being studied by various professional disciplines, including Psychology and Neurology. While anyone has yet to come up with a full understanding of exactly how the ability works, here are a few brief definitions:

Intuition[16]: The word comes from the Latin word *intuir*, which means "knowledge from within." Interestingly, extensive psychological testing has shown that while the conscious part of the person's brain doesn't seem to be involved, the tests show a significant amount of brain power being <u>used rapidly</u>. One amazing feature of intuition is that what the person senses is often <u>not based on anything their physical senses</u> can prove (usually just "knowing" something on the inside).

(1) A natural ability or power that makes it possible to know something without any proof or evidence.
(2) A feeling that guides a person to act a certain way without fully understanding why.
(3) Instinctive knowledge or belief.
(4) <u>Quick</u> and ready insight
(5) <u>Immediate</u> apprehension or cognition
(6) The power or faculty of attaining to direct knowledge or cognition without evident rational thought and inference.

---

[16] http://www,merriam-webster.com/.../intuition;
http://www.m.dictionary.com/definition/intuition and
http:www.thefreedictionary.com/intuition

(7) Insight – the ability to understand people and situations in a very clear way, and understand the "true" nature of something regardless of what it "looks" like.

(8) Direct perception of truth, fact, etc. independent of any reasoning process; immediate apprehension

(9) The act or faculty of knowing or sensing without the use of rational process.

Influence[17]:

There is a huge movement, especially in the marketing and business world, which is teaching techniques called, "The Influencer". The central theme of the movement is "The power to change anything." In the context that I am speaking, I am not talking about a set of techniques learned from an outside source, but I am talking about an inherent character that females have to be able to "woo" men, and persuade them. The God given purpose of it was to be a help to the man by influencing him to do positive things, such as stated earlier in the book. For example, veeery few men will spend an adequate amount of time at

---

[17] http:wwwgoogle.com./influence; http:www.merriam-webster.com/.../influence; http://www.m.dictionary.com/definition/influence

home with family, without some "suggestions" or persuasion from a woman.

    Nor are there many men will choose to get up in the middle of the night with a newborn, just for the sake of bonding with him, without a lot of encouragement from the woman. You may have one of the rare ones.
    Or how about this one? I believe that left on their own without any feminine influence in their lives, men would eventually have continual war until they kill everything alive.

(1) The power to change or affect someone or something without directly forcing them to happen.
(2) The ability to persuade or induce.
(3) To have an effect upon (actions, events, etc.)
(4) To have an effect on the condition or development of…
(5) The act or power of producing an effect without apparent exertion of force or direct exercise of command.
(6) Corrupt interference with authority for personal gain.
(7) Power exerted over the minds or behavior of others.
(8) A force exercised and received consciously or

unconsciously.

(9) The capacity or power of persons or things to be a compelling force on or produce the actions of.

Concerning the ability of feminine influence, the Bible is replete with examples of what can happen when a woman gets involved with helping (or coercing) a man into doing something, either for good or bad. Some positive examples include Abigail (I Sam 25), Esther, Ruth and Priscilla (Acts 18). Some negative examples include Sarah (Gen 16), Delilah (Judges 16) and the infamous Jezebel (I Kings).

If you're not fully convinced yet about the innate power of female influence, come watch the little 18-month-old baby girl who already knows how to turn it up. When Mommy says no, she turns those eyes onto Dad, with the big tears in them and says very emphatically, "Dad-dy. Daaaddy. Daad-ddy." If that doesn't work, she starts with the little baby girl whining, and in a few minutes, he goes down like a sack of potatoes.

When baby boy, who is only a little older, tries it, he gets sent to his room with an admonishment to "man up." Little girls grow up into big girls, and that ability to influence starts working early.

To my sisters: only use your intuition and influence for good, at the right time, and for the right reasons. God is watching you!!

Part Two

"Women's Wisdom"

See Appendixes added to the back of book with a smattering of issues that concern women, and information which may be helpful when talking to teenagers.

Chapter 11

"The Heart That Keeps Giving"

Having "The Heart that keeps giving" is not the problem for most women in general – God created us for that purpose and that is our very nature. However, *most of our problems come from not knowing what, when, and how much to give – and when enough is enough."*

Eve "gave" something from her heart, and she ended up naked, uncovered, ashamed, thrown under the bus by her man, and offered up by him as a sacrifice to save himself. Why?

She did what we, as women, often do with our men, our offspring, and everyone else around us - *she stepped beyond her legitimate boundaries*. We do that all the time, in the name of "giving from our heart."

We often continue to keep drawing water from an exhausted, overworked well within ourselves – until we become frustrated, bitter, angry, unforgiving, and poisoned by the knowledge that our men and children are not perfect. More often than not, they can be downright ungrateful and nasty.

These principles are the same for single women as for married women. God created us to be under the covering of a male in our lives *for as long as we live* – father, brother, son, Pastor, Deacon, friend, or neighbor who looks out for you, and etc. ***A woman with no caring male influence (positive) in her life is uncovered and vulnerable – it is against our nature.***

Nowadays, we call it "independence" – what it is really is spiritually naked and uncovered. Don't get mad with me – I am not the creator!! I've yet to see a scripture that instructs us to be more independent, either from men or God. Have you?

For those in ministry, we share the same Great Commission as male believers. We, then, feel compelled to maintain home and family, and yet find a way to participate in ministry. We try to find ways to give 150% out of our lives and then wonder why we become drained and exhausted.

We are often deluded enough to believe that we are as capable and fit as men are to physically maintain a certain schedule, and to prove that we can do it alone if necessary. Get real!!

As women, within ourselves we know that we are to be the nurturer and bearer of life, and so we keep giving and giving and giving – and doing and doing and doing – as if we are trying to make up for Eve giving Adam the tainted fruit. Stop the madness!!

Sisters, I challenge you to learn to back up and do "You" as God created and called us to be – helpers, not gods - in the lives of those around us. Go in the phone booth, take off the cape, and acknowledge that you do get tired sometimes. You do get bruised and broken by life, and even often by the very man who is supposed to cover you. Stop living like you are the "one size fits all". You are not the only answer for every situation. Only God can be all things to all people.

Married women, stop trying to be your husband's wife, mother, boss, mentor and supervisor all in one. Single women, stop trying to be the mother, father, boss, coach, and all-in-all to your children. That is a fallacy. You cannot be a father, only a good mother!! Ask God for wisdom to establish some boundaries. Prioritize your time, finances, duties, recreation, and etc.

Ask God to give you wisdom of what you actually are to do, what to delegate or what else to just not be involved with at all, ever!

Let's get our "perception" straight - learn to "help" – without needing to be the total answer to everything for everybody. I promise you; the world will not stop turning. Stop acting like a slave, and then screaming about being treated like one.

One more important thing for you to remember –Don't just be a "Heart that keeps on giving" - Learn to be a Heart that keeps on *for*giving. Forgive Tom and Jake and Harry and all the other Adams who have thrown you under the bus in your life (plus all of their little miniature Adams and Adam-ettes).

If you're married to an accuser or otherwise imperfect man, forgive him and ask God to help you love and "help" your man. You're not to be his savior and lord. Let me be veeeery clear; I'm not telling you to stay in an abusive situation!! If you're in one, seek help.

If you're single and hoping to be married one day, decide now that there is no un-fallen Adam on the table. Just know this, sooner or later he will throw you under the bus in some kind of way.

So work on becoming the woman that God wants you to be so that you'll be a help, "fit" for the right man. If you're "happily unmarried" and never want to be married, that's okay too. If your DNA is female, you're still a woman, regardless of your "sexual preference" or behavior. Your purpose is to still to nurture and protect life.

While my neck is on the line right here, let me go one step further. Of all the legal "rights" that God gave us as women, I have never seen anything in the Bible that includes the right to "abort" a life that has been conceived in your body. Do I condemn you? I certainly do not. I desire that you seek and find whatever help you need.

Moving on, our task is to ask God where He would have each of us to carry out His purpose for our lives. What are our functions, and who are the appropriate male coverings which God places in our lives?

Take the necessary times to replenish ourselves correctly with enough rest, and restorative "re-creation", i.e., designated weekends. That's why women's fellowships and conferences, and close relationships with other nurturers are sooooo essential for females.

They help to empower us to be "fit" to accomplish the purpose for which God has made us. No man can fully understand what it is like to be a woman, or fully understand how we think or feel. So, just let the buggers off the hook, and let God deal with them, while we learn to find our correct position in God.

If by chance you have a husband or man who is out of his correct position, stop talking to him about it. Talk to God, and begin to intercede to God on your man's behalf. First, ask God to fix you and then begin to agree with God for him in prayer that the will and purpose of God will manifest in his life. Are Eve's eyes seeing a little clearer yet?

CHAPTER 12

"Healing Through Forgiveness"

Just take a second to get pictures in your mind of your parents, spouse, children, friends, and anyone else whom you now have or have had a close relationship. Then when you get them in your mind, say this, "People are just human! God help us!"

Because we are people, we will often disappoint ourselves, our spouses, our children, our parents, God, and anyone else. But there is a confidence that we <u>can</u> have in the only being who can help us to overcome any and all of our hurts, hang-ups, habits, and challenges; and can still enable us to be the best person that we can be in this life.

In spite of rape or molestation, physical, mental, and emotional abuse, as well as abandonment, and on and on, He is the only one in whom we can put complete confidence. We can know that He will never fail or disappoint us.

Right in the middle of what we call "The Lord's Prayer" in Matt 5 is verse 12, "And forgive us our debt as we forgive our debtors". Then the point is reinforced in verses 14 + 15, where Jesus said, "For if you forgive men their trespasses, your Heavenly Father will also forgive you. But if you do not forgive men their trespasses; neither will your Father forgive your trespasses.

Let me use an example to show you what choosing forgiveness is like - it's like being out on the Titanic after being hit by a huge iceberg. As a result of the event, you find yourself floundering around in the dark sea of life broken, bruised, and screaming for help. You manage to find a broken piece of wood that is floating along, and you take hold of it to help you stay afloat.

You know that the little piece of wood is from the destroyed boat, but it's all you have to keep you afloat for the moment. While you are floating around helplessly, you realize how much you hate the ship that this piece of wood was a part of, and you would really like to maybe even say a few choice words about it. But you still need it to keep you going for now. Then miraculously, you see a light through the darkness, you hear a motor from a boat, and you hear someone yelling "Is anyone there who needs help?"

Finally the people who have come to rescue you find you hanging onto the piece of broken ship with both hands. They can't get close enough to you to pull you out of the water. So, they throw you a rope to grab hold to. You try to grab the rope for help, while still holding on to the piece of broken ship, but you don't have enough strength to do it with one hand. The rescuers are screaming to you, "Grab the rope. Let go of that old piece of rubbish, and grab the rope with both hands so we can pull you to safety."

At this point, we have a choice to hold on stubbornly to the broken piece of the ship of our life which has been totally devastated – or let it go and reach with both hands and everything in us for a new life. This will determine whether we will ever be able to receive and give real love, in spite of our horrible shipwrecks.

We did not choose to be abused or taken advantage of. We were powerless – but eventually we have the opportunity to take our power back, and to make a choice. We can choose to surrender the wound and the perpetrator to God, so that we can be rescued, healed, and delivered – or we can use the power of our choice to hold on to the filthy brokenness until we eventually drown and go under.

Let me just share a brief portion from my own life testimony, the impact that God will make in your life if you let Him. My parents separated when my Mom was three months pregnant with me, but she didn't realize it at first. Therefore, I was definitely not a wanted baby.

Long story short, my Dad kidnapped me and my two older brothers from my mother when I was just 5 years old, and my brothers were 6 and 7. We were placed under blankets and taken out of state. It was nine very long years later before I was given back to my Mom. By that time, I was an emotionally and physically abused 14-year-old, who but for the Grace and Love of God, would have been a total psychotic basket case.

During those nine years, we did not know where my Mom was, and she didn't know that my Dad had taken her babies thousands of miles away. We were almost constantly on the move. The story is long, and I've actually written 4 books to tell it. But I just want to say this – throughout all of those years, everywhere that I was taken to, I can reach back and remember how God always put someone around us who would invite my brothers and I to go to Sunday School and church.

Most of my immediate family members who raised me were not church goers. No one prayed with us at home. While staying for a brief time with my Dad's grandmother, I learned to say the "Now I lay me down to sleep" prayer, and how to sing her favorite hymn, "Rock of Ages". But I never saw any of the adults in my family go to church or read their Bible or pray.

Later, during really hard times, I would sing the song "Rock of Ages cleft for me, let me hide myself in Thee", and it would give me peace.

Your physical care of your child is not enough. When I was a child, I never knew a hungry day. We had nice things, the best that a middle-income family could provide for their children – which in those days was not bad.

My Dad was too busy living a social life, so he left us for long periods of time with his mother or with whoever the girlfriend was at the time. But there was not ever one single day that I remember my grandmother hugging me or my brothers and telling us that she loved us.

The worst of it was that by the time we were returned to my Mom at ages 14, 15 and 16, my Mom was unable to re-bond with us emotionally to ever show us the motherly love of a parent who has raised a child.

My oldest brother became an alcoholic before age 20 and remained one until he died at age 60. Although he accepted salvation before he died, he never experienced the more positive side of life.

My second brother followed him and became addicted to alcohol in his teens and later to hard drugs while in the Vietnam War and continues to be bound by addiction today.

Thanks be unto God that I learned about the love of God at age 19. By that time I was married to a gang war lord and drug dealer, and we had 3 children. I have survived inhumane beatings, rape, gang-wars, single parenting of 6 children and much more. But today I can say "Thank God" for the ropes thrown to me by people whom God strategically placed in my life to bring me up and out.

It took me some time, but the Lord gave me a revelation while I was praying one day. I was telling God how much I hated my Dad and his mother for taking us, and even my mother for not coming to find us. God gave me this nugget, "Each one of them did the very best they could do with what they had, who they were, and what they knew at that time. Given a different set of circumstances and understanding, they may have done differently."

That was the beginning of my finding my way to wholeness – you can make it too. It took me some time, and I went through a process, but I came to a place of forgiveness and peace about it.

I used various tools placed in my path including Christian counseling, journaling, seeking out a mentor and a lot of praying and reading the Bible. I learned that God is not the darkness. He is the light in the midst of the darkness.

If you can receive it – you can find healing for many of your wounds through "Forgiveness."

Chapter 13

"Emotions Are Not Just A Female Thang"

In the following section, I will address "emotionality" in general, and then more specifically, in terms of relationships. Because of my totally dysfunctional childhood, I have to continue to work at a personal commitment to be more attentive to how I relate to family and to others, in terms of "relationship". The greater the enlightenment to my "eyes of understanding"** about how we interact with one another, from a natural and a spiritual perspective; the more I have come to realize that every area of our lives is impacted by our associations with others.

One of the specific innate characteristics common to both woman and man is the phenomenon called "emotions". This powerful area of human experience is common to every living person, regardless of gender, race, religion, culture, socio-economic status, age, and etc. From birth to death emotions play a major part of all of our lives.

At the risk of being "run out of town on a rail" by some of my female comrades, I will venture to affirm that men actually do *experience and express* emotions, howbeit, not usually in the manner like we do!! Notice that I emphasize "experience and express", and that I did not say "verbalize". Let's begin by taking a look at the nature and origin of emotions, including scientific data, spirituality, and a Biblical perspective.

DEFINITION

One definition of **"Emotion"** is the complex psycho-physiological experience of an individual's state of mind as interacting with biochemical (internal) and environmental (external) influences. In humans, emotion fundamentally involves "physiological arousal, expressive behaviors, and conscious experience".[1] Emotion is associated with mood, temperament, personality, disposition, and motivation. The English word 'emotion' is derived from the French word *émouvoir*. This is based on the Latin *emovere*, where *e-* (variant of *ex-*) means 'out' and *movere* means 'move'.[2]

From this definition of emotions we could simply say that emotions are *"characteristics which every human being experiences both mentally and physically, and which are influenced internally within ourselves and/or by our external environment."* In other words, emotions affect us both inside and outside

A completely comprehensive dissertation on emotions is far beyond the scope or intent of this book, and not my primary focus. However, I do want to share enough information for us to realize that emotions are not just some little "hot flashes" or "hives", and definitely not just a "female thang". So ladies, the next time someone tritely says, "Oh, you're just being emotional"; you can say, "Yes, that is one of God's gifts to me."

COMMON EMOTIONS

Emotions are generally classified as either "primary" or "learned." A primary emotion is basic and instinctual, while a learned behavior tends to be more complex. Primary (instinctual) emotions usually disappear quickly and are replaced with secondary (learned).

For example, if a child is punished every time he writes on a wall, he fears (primary) punishment every time he engages in the behavior. In time he will feel guilt (secondary) which he has learned rather than the initial fear.

Here are the generally accepted definitions of the most common emotions, and you are more than likely to be surprised to realize that some of these are even considered as emotions:

>Affection = a "disposition or rare state of mind or body" that is often associated with a feeling or type of love.

>Anger = an emotion related to one's perception of having been offended or wronged and a tendency to undo that wrongdoing by retaliation

>Annoyance = an unpleasant mental state that is characterized by such effects as irritation and distraction from one's conscious thinking. It can lead to other emotions such as frustration and anger.

>Angst = an intense feeling of oppression, anxiety or inner turmoil

>Apathy = a state of indifference or the suppression of emotions such as concern, excitement, motivation and passion. An apathetic individual has an absence of interest in or concern about emotional, social, or physical life

>Anxiety = a psychological and physiological state characterized by somatic, emotional, cognitive, and behavioral components. The root meaning of the word anxiety is 'to vex or trouble'; in either the absence or presence of psychological stress, anxiety can create feelings of fear, worry, uneasiness and dread. Anxiety is considered to be a normal reaction to stress

>Awe = an emotion comparable to wonder but less joyous, and more fearful or respectful.

>Contempt = an intense feeling or attitude of regarding someone or something as inferior, base, or worthless—it is similar to scorn. It is also used when people are being sarcastic

>Curiosity = an emotion related to natural inquisitive behavior such as exploration, investigation, and learning.

>Depression = a state of low mood and aversion to activity that can affect a person's thoughts, behavior, feelings, and physical well-being. Characterized by a persistent and intense lowered mood, as well as disruption to one's ability to function in day-to-day matters.

>Desire = a sense of longing for a person or object or hoping for an outcome. Desire is the fire that sets action aflame.

>Despair = or **hopelessness** is the loss of hope. Some believe a person who experiences hopelessness will look to the future pessimistically

Disappointment = the feeling of dissatisfaction that follows the failure of expectations to manifest.

Disgust = an emotion that is typically associated with things that are regarded as unclean, inedible, infectious or otherwise offensive

Ecstasy = a subjective experience of total involvement of the person with an object of his or her awareness. Because total involvement with an object of our interest is not our ordinary experience and we are ordinarily aware also of other objects, the ecstasy is an example of <u>altered state of consciousness</u> characterized by diminished awareness of other objects or complete lack of the awareness of surroundings and everything around the object.

Empathy = the capacity to share the sadness or happiness of another sentient (responsive) being through consciousness rather than physically. Empathy <u>develops the ability to have compassion</u> towards other beings.

Envy = best defined as an <u>emotion</u> that "occurs when a person lacks another's *(perceived)* superior quality, achievement or possession and either desires it or wishes that the other lacked it."

Embarrassment = an <u>emotional</u> state experienced upon having a socially or professionally unacceptable act or condition witnessed by or revealed to others.

Euphoria = is <u>medically</u> recognized as a <u>mental</u> and <u>emotional</u> state defined as a profound sense of <u>well-being</u>.

Fear = a distressing emotion aroused by a perceived threat. It is a basic survival mechanism occurring in response to a specific stimulus, such as pain or the threat of danger

Frustration = is a common emotional response to opposition. Related to anger and disappointment, it arises from the perceived resistance to the fulfillment of individual will.

Gratitude = (**thankfulness, gratefulness or appreciation**) a positive emotion or attitude in acknowledgment of a benefit that one has received or will receive.

Grief = a multi-faceted response to loss, particularly to the loss of someone or something to which a bond was formed. This also has physical, cognitive, behavioral, social, and philosophical dimensions.

Guilt = occurs when a person realizes or believes—accurately or not—that he or she has violated a moral standard, and bears significant responsibility for that violation.

Happiness = a state of mind or feeling characterized by contentment, love, satisfaction, pleasure or joy.

Hatred = an intense feeling of dislike. Though not always, hatred is often associated with feelings of anger.

Hope = a belief in a positive outcome related to events and circumstances in one's life.

Horror = is the feeling of revulsion that usually occurs *after* something frightening is seen, heard or otherwise experienced. It is the feeling one gets after coming to an awful realization or experiencing a deeply unpleasant occurrence. Differs from terror because terror is the "extreme" sense of anxiety or dread "prior" to the event.

Hostility = a form of angry internal rejection or denial in psychology. In everyday speech it is more commonly used as a synonym for anger and aggression.

Hysteria = describes a state of mind of unmanageable emotional excesses. People who are "hysterical" often lose self-control due to an overwhelming fear.

Interest = a feeling or emotion that causes attention to focus on an object or an event or a process. Similar to curiosity.

Jealousy = typically refers to the negative thoughts and feelings of insecurity, fear, and anxiety over an anticipated loss of something that the person values, such as a relationship, friendship or love. Jealousy often consists of a combination of emotions such as anger, sadness, and disgust. It is not to be confused with envy

Joy = similar to happiness.

Loathing = same as hatred and disgust.

Love = the emotion of strong affection and personal attachment. In philosophical context, love is a virtue representing all of human kindness, compassion, and affection. In religious context, love is not just a virtue, but the basis for all being ("God is love"), and the foundation for all divine law (Golden Rule).

Lust = is an inordinate craving for carnal pleasure, which can sometimes assume a violent or self-indulgent character.

Misery = a feeling of great unhappiness, suffering, and/or pain.

Pity = evokes a tender or sometimes slightly contemptuous sorrow or empathy for people animals in misery, pain or distress.

Pride = is either (1) a high sense of one's personal status or ego (i.e., leading to judgments of personality and character) or (2) the specific mostly positive emotion that is a product of praise or independent self-reflection

<u>Rage</u> = a mental state that is one extreme of the intensity spectrum of <u>anger</u>. When a person experiences rage, it usually lasts until a threat is removed or the person under rage is incapacitated.

<u>Regret</u> = a negative conscious and <u>emotional</u> reaction to personal past acts and behaviors. Regret is often expressed by the term "*sorry*." Regret is often felt when someone feels <u>sadness</u>, <u>shame</u>, <u>embarrassment</u>, <u>depression</u>, <u>annoyance</u> or <u>guilt</u> after committing an action or actions that the person later wishes that he or she had not done.

<u>Remorse</u> = an emotional expression of personal <u>regret</u> felt by a person after he or she has committed an act which they deem to be shameful, hurtful or violent. Remorse is closely allied to <u>guilt</u> and self-directed <u>resentment</u>

<u>Sadness</u> = an <u>emotion</u> characterized by <u>feelings</u> of disadvantage, loss, helplessness, sorrow, and rage. When sad, people often become outspoken, less energetic, and emotional. It is a temporary lowering of <u>mood</u>.

<u>Shame</u> = The roots of the word shame are thought to derive from an older word meaning *to cover*; as such covering oneself, literally or figuratively, is a

natural expression of shame. Shame is a violation of cultural or social values while guilt feelings arise from violations of one's internal values. Thus, it is possible to feel ashamed of thought or behavior that no one knows about and to feel guilty about actions that gain the approval of others.

Shyness = the feeling of apprehension, lack of comfort or awkwardness experienced when a person is in proximity to, approaching or being approached by other people, especially in new situations or with unfamiliar people. Shyness may come from genetic traits, the environment in which a person is raised, and personal experiences.

Sorrow = classified as a primary emotion and has two *impulses*, to cling to the object of sorrow and to repair the injuries done to that object that caused the emotion in the first place. The primary emotion of sorrow is the basis for the emotion of pity.

Suffering = an individual's basic "feeling" experience of unpleasantness and aversion associated with harm or threat of harm. It may come in all degrees of intensity, from mild to intolerable

Surprise = a brief emotional state experienced as the result of an unexpected significant event. It can be neutral, pleasant or unpleasant. If a person experiences a very powerful or long-lasting surprise, it may be considered shock (can create strong physical responses).

Wonder = an emotion comparable to surprise that people feel when perceiving something very rare or unexpected (but not threatening). Also linked to curiosity.

Worry = thoughts and images of a negative nature in which mental attempts are made to avoid anticipated potential threats As an emotion, it is experienced as anxiety or concern about a real or imagined issue, usually personal.

Part Three

"Men Speak"

Chapter 14

"Not Right Now"

- Just as a man is fulfilled through "thinking" out the intricate details of solving a problem, a woman is fulfilled through "talking" about the details of the problems.
- When a man loves a woman, periodically he needs to pull away before he can get closer.
- When men and women are able to respect and accept their differences, then love has a chance to blossom.
- A woman's sense of self is defined through her feelings and the quality of her relationships. A man's sense of self is defined through his ability to achieve results.
- We mistakenly assume that if our partners love us, they will react and behave in certain ways - the ways we react and behave when we love someone.

Concerning the nature of the man having been created initially "alone", let me take a quick intermission from my Biblical focus to address something that has caused major grief in the lives of women for eons. I want to go back to some books that I mentioned earlier, for just a bit.

Many of you may remember the book I mentioned earlier titled, "Men Are From Mars and Women Are From Venus. One of the points raised by the author which is often an issue of contention for many couples – is the certain "need" which ALL adults of the male species seem to have in common – yes, according to research even in the animal kingdom among animals with higher intelligence.

I believe that Gray described it something like the "hibernating bear in a cave" tendency – which is often announced with some of these all too familiar phrases: "Can a man please get a break?"; "I'm going to my man cave"; "I need some alone time to think straight"; "I don't want to talk about it now"; "Not right now" or "Bug off!!"

Of course, the actual words and voice tone that announces the "demand" for a period of hibernation, largely depends on how long it has been since the last "cave" break. It may also depend on how much stress the man has been under just prior to the announcement. I feel safe to say that every adult woman who has lived with an adult man for more than a week has had this experience – whether husband, son, father, brother, and etc.

The point that Gray was making is that **this occurrence is not to be taken as a direct insult or personal affront by the woman. This is a part of the internal nature of the man -** it doesn't mean that he doesn't love you during those times. (It also doesn't mean that it doesn't suck!!) Rather, that he can't stand to be around you or anybody else (except strangely, another male) until he's had time to "regroup". *Did I hear a thousand women say, "Yeah Right?"*

In the book titled, "Dare to Be Called a Man", Bishop Evans describes an intrinsic quality that he believes all men have, a quality which he terms, "Omni". It's not the divine "Omni" as only Creator God has (omnipotence, omnipresence, and omniscience), but the "human" quality of Omni (as in the "image and likeness" of God).

Not to quote Bishop exactly, but the gist of his discussion is to help women understand how men can stay away from us for lengths of time, and not feel the need to connect every so often. I believe that almost every women who lives in a civilized environment has experienced the frustration of having their husband or significant male tell them, "I'll call you later or in a little bit"; only to have them not call for hours, or even days. Usually, it's way past the time that she expects the call. It's because we work under a totally different concept of time.

Of course, when a woman is told to expect a call by "6 o' clock", we are definitely waiting near the phone by "5:55" so as not to miss it. Not only that, but we are even gracious enough to allow a 5-minute grace period. However, by "6:06" with no call, we start panicking. "Surely, something bad has happened, like a fatal accident, so he can't get to a phone."

Then, by "7:00" with no call, a little anger starts to build in, along with the anxiety. By "7:15", he is no longer half dead, but is in the bed with some floozy. God forbid that it be "7:30", when he calls. He is going to hear at least 5 minutes of why, where, how, what and who, before we even say "Hi".

Let's not even talk about the man who is supposedly meeting us some place at a certain time, but arriving late or not showing at all. (This wreaks such emotional trauma to think about, that it could take up the entire rest of this book).

Suffice it to say, the "Omni" principle is probably at work, according to Bishop.

The gist of it (in my own words) is that Adam was created alone, with a sense of having everything that he needed within himself (sense of being self sustaining, with just him and God, alone). That nature remains inherent in every man until present time. The positive side of this trait is why men, generally speaking, can go away for long periods of time to hunt, work and war without falling apart in their psyche and emotions.

Can you imagine the hunter out searching for food to sustain his family turning back with empty hands because he can't stand being away from home and woman? How about a warrior who is distracted, thinking about his woman while in fierce combat with an enemy? How about the "bum" (I mean player) who can't stand to leave his woman long enough to go to work? As with most things in life, there is a positive and a negative side.

Man has the ability to function without having to be constantly physically affirmed by the woman – **as long as she treats him good when he is in her presence, the awareness of that stays with him and sustains him.**

Women, on the other hand, **were never created to be alone, and self sustaining** – that is why we are constantly seeking reaffirmation from a man. As soon as the man's physical presence is absent and the sound of his voice is no longer in our ears, we feel "alone" and like a piece of us is missing:

- "Do you love me?" (*Didn't I tell you that yesterday?*) "But do you love me today?" (*Why do I need to tell you that I love you again today?*) "I just want to hear you say it." (*But I already said it.*)
- "Hi honey, just called to say "Hi". (*Okay honey, but this is the 4th time you've called me since I got to work and it's only 10:00 a.m.*). "I know honey, but I just wanted to hear your voice." (*Okay, talk to you later.*) "Okay, call me on your lunch break."
- "Honey, are we still going to church tonight?" (*Dag, I told you "yes" before I left home. I'm not even at work ye***t**.)
- "Honey, do you think I'm still pretty?" (*Yes, you're beautiful*) "Aw, you don't mean that. You're just saying it. Do you reeeeally think so?" (*Yes honey, talk to you later*). "What's wrong with me that you don't want to talk to me for a few minutes? Are you losing interest in me?" (*Baby, I'm still at work*) "I

don't think you really love me anymore. Bye!" Click

That is why, generally speaking, women need to form close bonds with girl friends (fan clubs); to help affirm one another. We need help to fill in the gaps with discussions and talks to share things. Takes the pressures off husbands/boyfriends who don't feel like taking hours to listen to you talk about "illogical", emotional stuff.

If you want to know what real frustration is, try to turn your husband into a girlfriend, with whom you can share every little detail about home and nest, i.e., "What's your favorite brand of soap?" or "I'm having one of those "PMS" days." or "Who has milk on sale this week?" or "What color should I dye my hair?"

Chapter 15

"Men Wish Women Understood"

In this section, I share some information that comes from a weekly radio broadcast that I produced and hosted called "Dew Tell". My theme and purpose of the broadcasts was "to help build and strengthen family relationships. In light of my childhood, I have always carried a desire and vision to help build healthy families.

I asked the men in our radio audience to respond to the above question and here are some of the responses which we received. The survey included a cross section of men of varying ages, marital status, and geographical locations.

"I wish that my woman would understand that it's very challenging to admit to her when I make mistakes because I don't think she'll be empathetic."

"That it's okay for me to receive praises at least once in a while. Even God loves to be praised and appreciated, not that I'm equating myself to God. There is a real power in praising your man."

"Manhood" is usually painted as being machismo, but we do have a delicate and sensitive side too. We should be able to feel free to express our emotions, and not worry about appearing weak or vulnerable. Encouragement gets way better results."

"We are simple, but different, not really complicated. I love praises and compliments too. I can still be a "real" man and be sensitive."

"We're raised to protect women, but we also need to be nurtured, but not like little kids."

"God is the Lord of Hosts (Battle), but He is also Love. We like to be able to change, but not appear to be like a woman."

"All men are not dogs." "We can be romantic."

"Men are simple, and do what works. Oftentimes sisters reward "dog-like" behavior; and good guys may only get 1 or 2 real girlfriends in their whole lives."

"Women can change a man's dog-like behavior by not accepting it. Don't make wrong choices to avoid delayed gratification. Don't be influenced by the macho images on TV."

"Everything that seems to work is not right."

"It's not right for women to use our children as weapons against us after a break-up. They often become bitter and oppositional."

"I need for women to understand that communication is a real problem for me. The ability to listen needs to be put in context."

"Marriage is a spiritual relationship too, and the enemy of our soul is attacking every relationship (vertical and horizontal)."

"The devil hates all human unions (relationships) and does anything to inflame flesh and weaknesses."

****

"What Can You Do To Change You To Help Improve The Relationship?"

"Regarding communications, don't read hidden interpretations. Take words at face value. Don't talk when she's talking. Try not to shut down when she argues or screams."

"I think men and women speak two different languages, and could use an interpreter at times. I need to try to hear what is being said – not just the words, but the real meaning."

"We need to study the woman, and get to "really" know her."

"I need to work to share what is on my heart, instead of clamming up or shutting down."

"I'll work on considering the bigger picture, change myself and also study her to help address her needs."

"I need to learn how to respond differently, and work on the power of agreement.

"Have to change wrong thinking – in hindsight, can see errors in how I reacted based on wrong thinking. Will seek to obtain the mind of Christ, and to share with like-minded brothers."

"I need to return back to being a gentleman, open doors, take off hat, teach young men about chivalry and don't whistle or degrade women."

"We need to use the same effort as when courting, to maintain and excel in gentleman's qualities and actions."

"Work harder and use more effort when children are on board."

"Study spouse's love language and how to nurture them."

"Learn how to court even when responsibilities have overwhelmed, and communications are so damaged."

"Have to do self introspection of how you love and treat yourself. Still "pursue" your wife/woman."

"Pray for wisdom and ways to keep the fire going."

"I believe what Malcolm X said, "That every man should know what a pimp knows about a woman, and every woman should know what every whore knows about a man."

"We shouldn't be defeated, but be prayerful and hopeful."

"Be more conscious of health and of taking care of myself and proper diet. Address the natural and the spiritual."

"The body is the temple of the Holy Spirit, and should not be treated like it sinful."

"Include your spouse in your "self care" time.

"May need counseling if the wife is not ready to be in marriage or doesn't want to be on the same page."

"Changing my behavior may bring change in the other person."

"May not know how to reach out on my own."

"I have to be courageous and strong."

"I have to work on timelines and procrastination, and be more prompt on calling wife when I'm supposed to. Respect spouse's power."

"Learn how to "respond" instead of how to "react". Decrease negative consequences.

Chapter 16

"Can Trust Be (Re) Built?"

"Be honest. Don't lie. Show interest in what she is interested in, especially during conversation."

"Spend more time together, talking and doing things together. Build confidence in one another."

"Help communications by doing things together, talking openly. See where each one really wants to go in the relationship. Be honest, truthful, and open."

"Honest relationships have to be built on consideration." Show interest in what they are doing."

"Be dependable and consistent."

"Consistency, especially in intimacy. Be sincere about how you feel and changes over time, such as likes and dislikes."

"Separate from those who dislike our spouses."

"Keep communication open, while setting time aside."

"It's not easy to rebuild a relationship but you can try to reintroduce yourself; try to reassure them that it won't happen again, and do everything in your power to try to make it right. Be patient."

"Work on real forgiveness, and try to rebuild confidence in your word."

"Work hard to have person regain confidence in you."

"Trust more in the Lord to repair the relationship."

"Remember it's a two-way street, and it needs time to be honest and open. Sacrifice the things you were doing which caused the break."

"Confess, repent, and allow God time to heal. See it like the analogy of our relationship with Christ."

"Be patient with spouse in the process, in spite of discouragement or time span."

"Be able to identify the problem or source of issues and remove it. If an issue comes back up, you must work together to face it."

"About the Author"

September is an accomplished author and Kappa Alpha Psi Literary Honoree. She is blessed to be Mom and Mom-Mom to a wonderful family.

There are so many facets to her person and life that it's amazing that one person could have experienced it all in just one lifetime. September is a celebrated author, entrepreneur, counselor, Pastor, Psychiatric R.N., motivational speaker, and producer of the previously aired *"Dew Tell"* Radio show and TV show, *"Ordinary People, Extraordinary God."*

She has a ready smile, quick wit, and a zest for living. Well known for her depth of love for people, September has a quick sense of humor, a "down to earth" perspective, and a faith-based worldview.

When asked what her primary life focus is, her watchword is **"Relationship"**. As the result of almost complete disintegration of her own birth family, she has a particular passion for helping others to strengthen family bonds.

September writes in a manner which causes the reader to feel present in the moment. Her style is conversational rather than formal, as if she were having a face-to-face visit with you. Her readers have commented that they have laughed, cried, cussed, and then repented while reading her books.

~ Other Books by Author ~

"September's Trilogy" is a powerful, dramatic and inspiring autobiography. Kidnapped at the age of 5, with 2 older brothers, September's story traverses through years of isolation, physical and emotional abuse, being moved place to place, gang-war violence, teen marriage to a gang warlord, single parenting, and much more. Previously published in the three separate books below, **"September's Trilogy"** includes the full story. This is not "based" on a true story, but is indeed fully true, howbeit often incredulous.

"While the Dew is Still on the Roses" (2007)

"He Tells Me I Am His Own" (2008)

"The Joy We Share As We Tarry There" (2009)

Get your copy today and get ready for an amazing journey.
ISBN-13: 978-0982684139
PAGES: 286
DIMENSIONS: 0.6" x 9" x 6"
LANGUAGE: English
FORMAT: Trade Paperback
PUBLISHED: 2010
Available at amazon.com (In Paperback or Kindle), barnesandnoble.com or www.september-summer.com
Connect with "September Summer" on Facebook, Twitter, LinkedIn

APPENDIX

Appendix A

FOUR TYPES OF LOVE

Storge - Affection

Affection (**storge**, στοργή) is fondness through familiarity, especially between family members or people who have otherwise found themselves together by chance. It is described as the most natural, emotive, and widely diffused of loves. Natural in that it is present without coercion; emotive because it is the result of fondness due to familiarity; and most widely diffused because it pays the least attention to those characteristics deemed "valuable" or worthy of love. As a result, it is able to transcend most discriminating factors. Ironically, its strength is also what makes it vulnerable. Affection has the appearance of being "built-in" or "ready-made", says Lewis. As a result, people come to expect, or even to demand, its presence—irrespective of their behavior and its natural consequences.

Phileo - Friendship

Friendship is a strong bond existing between people who share common interest or activity. Lewis explicitly says that his definition of friendship is narrower than mere companionship:

Eros - Romance

Eros (ἔρως) is love in the sense of 'being in love'. This is distinct from sexuality, which Lewis calls Venus, although he does spend time discussing sexual activity and its spiritual significance in both a pagan and a Christian sense. He identifies Eros as indifferent. It is Venus that desires the sexual aspect of a relationship, while Eros longs for the emotional connection with the other person.

Agape - Unconditional Love

Charity (**agapē**, ἀγάπη) is the love that brings forth caring regardless of circumstance. Lewis recognizes this as the greatest of loves and sees it as a specifically Christian virtue. The chapter on the subject focuses on the need of subordinating the natural loves to the love of God, who is full of charitable love.

Appendix B

"RELATIONSHIPS – THE SPICE OF LIFE"

I. **Human Relationship**
   A. Basic Definition - ***The position of a person to God first and then to one or more persons in a system.*** The system can be set in the boundaries of marriage and family, or it can be any number of different settings in society. The word relationship is actually the name of the system that those very positions make up. For example, when we talk about water, we don't usually call it the individual chemicals which the water is consisted of, which we know is h^2o- we just call it water. That's how it is with the word relationship – we don't usually say or even clearly think it through, that it actually has to do with at least two persons in a certain **_position_** to one another. Some things just take for granted.
   B. Example: That's why it's commonly understood language to say that when a man and woman have sexual intercourse, we say they've had relationship with one another – whether legally or illegally. However, when one person masturbates, it is subconsciously clear in our minds without even really thinking about it, that it is not called having "relationship" with yourself. Right now I am not speaking about the theological implications of the act of the individual, but

I am using that to show that *one person in a system does not make up a relationship.* The amazing thing is that even though this is not something that we normally thoroughly think about in terms of the word "relationship" – God has placed within mankind the intrinsic understanding that one cannot have "relationship" alone.

C. By definition – in every relationship, the state of being, the benefits or drawbacks, the responsibilities within, the satisfaction the joys and the sorrows, and etc. of each person is directly impacted by their position with regard to the other person or persons. For example – who is dominant at any given time (whether overtly or covertly)? Within this system of positions between people, decisions are made continually – decisions like: (1) Is my concern and affection more for the other person than for my own self? (2) Am I willing to let this person or persons see that I love them or care for them, and thereby make myself vulnerable to them? (3) Can I surrender this particular issue for the sake of our relationship, or do I force the issue even if it means doing damage to our relationship? (4) How important is it that I have to be the one who is right all or most of the time? (5) I know it is better to give than to receive in church – but does that include giving kindness to this person who may or may not show their appreciation? (6) Do we always have to agree to live together in peace and love? (7) Do I choose to have my own way regardless of how the other person feels? (8) What if I show them too much love, won't they try to take advantage? (9) I've been hurt or taken advantage of before – can I trust this person? (10) I don't want to agree because then it will look like I'm giving in. Won't that make me look like a weakling? (11) What would God want me to do? Or better yet (12) Do I even want to know what God wants me to do?

D. In human relationships there is no such thing as "true equality" because of how God created man. Man was created in the image and likeness of God, which by nature makes him "dependent" on someone outside of himself. First and foremost, in "position" – or relationship, man is dependent on the one who he is the image and likeness of. For example – your image in the mirror is dependent upon the presence of your physical body in order for the image to be visible. If you remove your physical body from in front of the mirror, your image will no longer be present. If you view yourself in certain types of mirrors, like the ones in amusement parks, your position or relationship with your image will be distorted. As it is in the natural, so it is in the spiritual - when a human being does not see himself in the true reflection of who God created him to be, his position or relationship with God and other humans becomes distorted. Some people see themselves as unworthy of love, from God or other humans – others think they deserve to be loved, but don't have to love in return. Truly healthy relationships come from taking a position somewhere in between the two extremes.

E. Since we are created in the image of, and are a little lower than Elohim as in Psa. 8, we are never in position or relationship with another human being as truly co-equal. Pure equality is an essence of divine nature, which only God has. There will always be a jockeying of position because sooner or sooner differences of opinion will arise, and a decision will ultimately have to be made. Usually what happens in healthy relationships is that a decision is made that will be include some of each person's opinion. But, none-the-less, there will still have to be an acquiescing of some ground for the sake of the relationship.

II. **In a Nutshell - Challenges to Relationship**

A. God created man in an already prepared environment – one in which God set Adam up so that he had everything he needed to be sustained physically and spiritually. God created Adam in relationship to his God upon whom he was dependent, and then gave to Adam relationship with his environment over which Adam was to be dominant.

B. Once that phase was complete, God put into place the completion of the Master plan. It was not in hindsight that God said, "It is not good that man should be alone" – God was simply doing what He always did with everything else -speaking into existence in the physical realm that which had already been eternally in God. God did not have a sudden revelation that man needed a helpmeet – *God created Adam to have a helpmeet,* someone to be in position or relationship with Adam.

C. If man was created in the image or likeness of the triune God, who was not alone but is in position to one another in one Godhead with the same divine nature, how could man possibly be created without a need for him to be in relationship with someone of like nature? God simply stated what was a reality based on Adam's nature – not a sudden revelation to God.

D. Here is the challenge – in this day and time that we live in, the enemy of our soul is working overtime to do what he began in the Garden of Eden- to distort our position or relationship to God first, and then to one another. **The enemy hates us for having the potential to be in a loving relationship with God and with one another.**

E. Jesus said, from the beginning it was God's will for man and woman to remain in relationship. Because of the hardness of the heart, those positions are broken. Again I'm not talking theologically about divorce – I'm talking about what cause broken human relationships of all types, and in particular, within families. It is because we are failing to see what our true positions are to be to one another. Most Christians don't have a problem getting into position or relationship with God, but it's the human ones we struggle with – the ones within our homes and families.

III. **The Obligation to Strengthen the Family from a Biblical Perspective**
   A. Jesus said, "If I be lifted up from the earth, I'll draw all men unto me." My question to you is, "draw all men unto Him" to do what? I am not just talking philosophically or theologically; I am talking day to day realistically.
   B. As Christians, it is not enough to be and teach how to be reconciled and in right position or relationship with God; we must pray and ask God to empower us to become instruments to be and to teach others to be reconciled and in right position/relationship with our family first and then with others.

IV. **Tidbits of Information about the Relationship of man to woman**
   A. For Married Folk or Singles Desiring Marriage:
      1. For a man to be suitable for marriage, the man's position must first begin as Adam's did, with God first. Only after the man brings an acceptable offering unto God will God have "respect" for the offering and the man (*Gen 4:4 "And Abel, he also brought of the firstlings of*

his flock and of the fat thereof. And the LORD had respect unto Abel **and** to his offering).* Only then, will the man be in position to receive the "Eve" that God will form for him.

2. When the man is in his rightful place, then the woman will be able to get in her rightful position or relationship with him as described in Ephes. 5:22 *"Wives, submit yourselves unto your own husbands, as unto the Lord."*
3. The Godly woman's relationship to her husband then will be directly positioned, or related to, based on vs. 23-24 *"For the husband is the head of the wife, even as Christ is the head of the church: and he is the Saviour of the body. Therefore as the church is subject unto Christ, so [let] the wives [be] to their own husbands in everything."*
4. Then and only then can the cycle be completed when in vs. 25, *"Husbands, love your wives, even as Christ also loved the church, and gave himself for it;* (There's that first fruit offering again, only this time it is himself that must be sacrificed)
5. Married couples must not connect just because they are physically attracted to one another or because they are emotionally needy. They are to connect because of the destiny and purpose of God for their spouse. Don't just look at the "now", but be willing to give out of

the will of God for you. Be willing to water into one another's life from the place of respect for the husband, and the place of favor for the wife.

B. <u>Single Men</u> - God will not give a godly woman a husband who has not earned God's respect first. You have to show God that you are able to cherish and properly manage the "favor" that will come with God's gift of the woman to you.

C. <u>Single Women</u> – You will only get the quality of a man to the degree of the living "well of favor" that resides in you. If your well is polluted with bitterness, unreleased anger or unforgiveness, the man that will be drawn to you will be of the same type as insects to manure. Ask God to purify and keep purified your "well". Prov. 4:23 *"Keep thy heart with all diligence; for out of it [are] the **issues** of life."*

Appendix C

RELATIONSHIP BUILDING

DEFINITION:

1. **connection:** a significant connection or similarity between two or more things, or the state of being related to something else
2. **behavior or feelings toward somebody else:** the connection between two or more people or groups and their involvement with one another, especially as regards the way they behave toward and feel about one another
3. **friendship:** an emotionally close friendship, especially one involving sexual activity

Relationship Stages of Development[3]

Relationship stages follow a predictable developmental process. It is important to remember that whether or not the relationship fully develops depends on the investment of each partner - it doesn't "just happen".

In fact, most relationships don't make it to the final stage and very few make it to the third stage. According to divorce statistics less than half make it out of the second stage. Healthy Relationships take work.

Stages of a healthy Relationship

Human growth and development occurs in stages - We refer to them as developmental stages. There are developmental stages for every important aspects of being human:

- Stages of Childhood
- Stages of Adolescence
- General Life Stages
- Stages of a Healthy Relationship

We use these stages as a compass to mark where we are in the process of growth. We can also have some idea of what to expect... or what's "normal" in a healthy relationship for a specific stage of growth.

You may be interested to know that each of the developmental processes listed above fit into stages of one specific, predictable, and recurring developmental process... They are "**stages-within-stages**" if you will.

These higher-level stages are:

- **Healthy Codependence**
    - *Childhood* - Infancy, codependent with mother during infancy.
    - *Adolescence* - Individuation, codependent with peer group or a romantic involvement.
    - *General Life Stages* - Generally codependent during childhood
    - *Long-Term Relationship Stages* - Healthy Codependence during courtship
    -
- **Healthy Counter-Dependence**
    - *Childhood* - Toddler, counter-dependent... "terrible two's".
    - *Adolescence* - Separation, counter-dependent with family
    - *General Life Stages* - Generally counter-dependent during adolescence years
    - *Long-Term Relationship Stages* - Healthy counter-dependence during Disillusionment & Conflict stage
- **Independence**

- *Childhood* - Pre-school, more able to play away from mother.
- *Adolescence* - Rebellion, helps break childhood bonds
- *General Life Stages* - Young adulthood, out on their own
- *Long-Term Relationship Stages* - My Life, Your Life, Our life...Stops blaming spouse having established healthy boundaries

- **Interdependence**
  - *Childhood* - School-aged, getting along with peers and learning how to be part of a group
  - *Adolescence* - Cooperation begins to cooperate with the world by working together with others to reach personal goals.
  - *General Life Stages* - Middle Adulthood to Wisdom
  - *Long-Term Relationship Stages* - Intimacy, can finish each other's sentences while maintaining sense-of-self

Each period of life represents the degree of separation one is able to establish... each developmental period is also an opportunity to rework separation issues from the previous period.

If a child is not allowed to establish enough separateness by the end of the infancy period, it sets the stage for unhealthy codependency in all the other stages. Internalizer is another term for unhealthy Codependent.

If a child is not allowed to establish enough separation by the end of the toddler stage, it can lead to problems with unhealthy counter-dependency in all the other stages. Externalizer is another term for unhealthy Counter-dependent.

John Bradshaw outlines 4 "General Periods" of a long-term, healthy relationship stages...

- **INFATUATION** - This is the "Honeymoon" or courtship period. It's a time when the biological processes involved with procreation are most pronounced.

  Bradshaw points out that this is when the brain is being bathed in testosterone, dopamine, and other internal feel-good chemicals... Some people even report feeling dizzy or like their head is spinning during this stage.

  There is a healthy codependency as the two merge emotionally into one... this over-connection is intoxicating. They may want to spend all their time together... can't stop thinking about each other, and etc. In this period it may actually be "cute" to notice that your new partner has a habit of leaving the cap off the toothpaste.

  Since the feelings are so strong, there is a tendency to idealize the other person. "No one else can make me feel this way". There is peace and harmony because your new mate "can do no wrong." But eventually the chemical bath subsides - usually in three to six months - it paves the way for disillusionment and conflict...

- **DISILLUSIONMENT & CONFLICT** - In this stage the balloon bursts and reality sets in as our biochemistry returns to its normal steady-state. **Now I suddenly realize that leaving the cap off the toothpaste really bugs me... It's not cute anymore and I don't have to take it!**

  Even healthy relationships go through this period of conflict early on. It's a time when neural networks are being updated and new ones created in order to adjust to living with someone. There is an instinctive jockeying for position in the newly forming status-quo. Just remember...it's a normal relationship stage and "this too will pass".

The fighting in this stage is healthy counter-dependency... It's healthy because it helps us to separate a bit from the over-connectedness of courtship.

Major life changes always bring on extra stress...even good changes. When we are under ongoing stress, the "fight-or-flight" response can be triggered easily and often.

If we are aware that this relationship stage is normal, it's much easier to work through. If we are unaware, then we might wake up one morning and say..."Oh...my God! What have I gotten myself into?" (isn't it interesting how we automatically want to pray when we're in trouble?)

In this relationship stage, we have gathered a list of negative things about our partner that we "never noticed before". It's a good time to remember this statement..."Whoever you are in a relationship with says as much about you as it does them."

I mean this as a reminder of what I refer to as the subconscious synchronization of compatible neural networks... When we "click" with someone, it is because our "Love Maps" mesh with each other on a conscious AND a subconscious level. (By the way, if you were aware of that it wouldn't be subconscious)

- **"MY LIFE, YOUR LIFE, OUR LIFE"** - If we make it to this stage, we have a good chance of staying in it for the long haul. This is where we establish healthy boundaries - **a balance of**

separateness and connectedness. I have my life, you have your life, and we have our life.

We have pretty much accepted most of the blemishes of our partner and love them anyway. People in a healthy relationship can do that you know - love someone even though they don't like some things about them. It's called differentiation and it is a sign that you are very close to true intimacy.

- **INTIMACY** - This is the most elusive of the relationship stages. In my opinion <u>true intimacy is the ability to share who you really are with another person. This implies they are able to share who they really are with you.</u>

The relationship stage of Intimacy may take up to 15 or 20 years to develop... depending on the investment both of you make in your relationship. In this stage you know each other so well that you can finish each other's sentences... but you still enjoy talking to each other anyway.

<u>Longevity is no guarantee that a couple can achieve intimacy... there have been many people married for 25 or more years who never really knew one another.</u>

If you have grown up in a less than nurturing home, then you may have trouble with this one. You must have access to your True-Self before you can share it with another. It may help to read all four parts of the "Iceberg."[18]

---

[18] http://www.internet-of-the-mind.com/relationship_stages.html

Appendix D

The Knapp's Relational Development Model[19]

Process Stage   **Representative Dialogue**

Coming Together

Stage	Dialogue
Initiating	"Hi, how ya doin'?" "Fine, you?"
Experimenting	"Oh, so you like to ski...so do I." "You do?! Great. Where do you go?"
Intensifying	"I...I think I love you." "I love you too."
Integrating	"I feel so much a part of you." "Yeah, we are like one person. What happens to you happens to me."

---

[19] http://www.en.wikipedia.org.../Knapp's_Relational_Model

Bonding	"I want to be with you always" "Let's get married."	

Coming Apart

Differentiating	"I just don't like big social gatherings." "Sometimes I just don't understand you. This is one area where I am not like you at all."	
Circumscribing	"Did you have a good time on your trip?" "What time will dinner be ready?"	
Stagnating	"What's there to talk about?" "Right, I know what you're going to say and you know what I'm going to say."	
Avoiding	"I'm so busy, I don't know if I'll be able to see you." "If I'm not around when you try, you'll understand."	

| Terminating | "I'm leaving you...and don't bother calling me." "Don't worry." |

The ***Knapp's Relational Development Model*** *is a theoretical model to map the progression of an <u>interpersonal relationship</u> between two parties. The Relational Development Model identifies 10 different stages divided into three overlapping phases: coming together, relational maintenance, and coming apart. To better understand what makes relationships work or fall apart, it is important to examine each stage of development not only by itself but also in its role in the movement from one stage to another as the relationship progresses or falls apart. It is important to note that movement is not necessarily progressive. It is possible to jump between the different phases.*

COMING TOGETHER PHASE

The first stage of the Coming Together phase of the Relationship Development Model is the **INITIATION STAGE** where first impressions of the two people involved in the relationship are made one the initial contact has been made. Often physical factors play a role in this stage, such as clothing, perfumes or colognes, hair styles, and overall appearance. People often want to **portray themselves as easy to talk to, friendly, and open to discussion**. This stage does not include deep revealing conversations, but rather light conversation meant to survey the possibility of a closer personal relationship with someone.

Moving from the initiation stage of the Model, the next stage is **EXPERIMENTATION**. In this stage of the relationship, the two people attempt to find some **common ground** between each other's lives such as common interests and hobbies. This stage is also referred to as the probing stage. Each person probes the other for information that would allow them to further the social connection between them. Many relationships end here, never developing to anything more than a mere acquaintance.

However, those relationships that do move to the next stage experience THE **INTENSIFYING** STAGE. Here also is where people **test the potential of the relationship with varying degrees of self disclosure** to see if that will be reciprocated and to test the impressions one is making. In the intensifying stage of the Relationship Development Model, relationships grow, and self-disclosure becomes more apparent and deep. People find many different ways to foster their relationships in order to stimulate relational development. Methods include giving gifts, asking for a romantic relationship commitment or expressing affection both verbally and nonverbally. Of course, there are no set guidelines for every relationship in the intensifying stage. Every relationship possesses unique characteristics that make it difficult for the Relationship Development Model to accurately predict if efforts to further the relationship will succeed or fail. Partners in some relationships may "test the waters" to see if particular advances are welcomed or frowned upon. These "secret" tests are intended to test the intensity of a relationship. They can include presenting the other person as a girlfriend or boyfriend (presentation) or seeing if the relationship lasts when a temporary physical separation between the two people occurs. Others will openly engage interpersonally in a declaration to the other of their intent to be exclusive in some fashion.

The fourth stage of relationship growth is the **INTEGRATION** stage, where **the lives of the two people begin to merge and their status as a couple is confirmed**. In this stage friends that one would have individually meet and social groups combine. Also occurring at this stage are the beginnings of a sexual relationship (in non-Christian relationships) and the deepest levels of self-disclosure are approached, signifying the intimacy of the relationship.

After the integration stage, the final stage of the coming together half of the Relationship DM is reached, the **BONDING** Stage. In this stage, the commitment of the relationship is communicated to the rest of the world. From a Biblical perspective, it could lead to marriage, but marriage is not necessary in the bonding stage. The bonding stage is where many intimate (in marriage) and romantic relationships remain indefinitely, until divorce, death, or otherwise. **Key points to maintaining a relationship at this stage include sharing power equally, emphasizing positive and constructive communication patterns, and making frequent connections with one another.**

COMING APART PHASE

Unfortunately, or fortunately depending on how you look at it, many relationships move from the coming together stages to the coming apart stages. Just as with the "coming together" stages, there are five stages of the coming apart. Ideally, the overwhelming difference within the relationship will be recognized PRIOR to marriage, such as during effective marriage counseling. The first stage of dissolving the relationship is the **DIFFERENTIATING** stage. During this stage of the Relationship Development Model, differences are exploited instead of the commonalities of the experimenting and intensifying stage. **The momentum of the "work together" attitude quickly shifts directions and becomes more individualistic.** Some may describe feelings of being held down and resentful of their commitment to their partner. **Temporary separation is a common solution to this stage of the relationship.**

Following the differentiating stage is the **CIRCUMSCRIBING** stage. In the circumscribing stage, the primary focus of the relationship shifts from differences to setting limits and boundaries on communication between the two people. The communication becomes much shallower, and the range of topics significantly decline. Partners may fear discussing deep topics because of the threat of a conflict. This may lead to less communication altogether.

If the decline of the relationship continues, it is likely to enter the third stage, **STAGNATION**. This stage builds off many of the problems of the circumscribing stage; communication **becomes more limited and less frequent. Stagnating relationships do not grow or progress but rather invoke a feeling of "nothing changes".**

The second to last stage of the dissolution of the relationship is the **AVOIDANCE** stage. **This stage takes the limited communication to a physical level.** Partners may avoid each other altogether, desiring separation from one another.

The final stage of the RDM is the **TERMINATION** stage. The relationship stops completely. **Although it is possible to save a relationship from this stage of development, it is very difficult to "relight the fire" that once held the relationship together.** However, the coming apart stages of the Relationship Development Model are not necessarily negative. Sometimes, it is healthy for two people to terminate their relationship in the interest of personal aspirations and well being. (Again, we pray this is determined during the dating or engagement periods). The Model cannot accurately describe all relationships, each relationship moves at different speeds and is affected by the personalities and communication abilities of the people involved.

Appendix E

Stages of Committed Relationships

By Sarah Shultz[20]

Have you ever wondered: *Why is our relationship so hard? Things were so perfect when we first met - what happened?* Most likely, the answer is that you've left the first stage of your relationship, and have moved into another. But could it really be that easy?

Yes! Most people understand that relationships grow and change over time... but what many people don't know is that they tend to evolve in the same way. There are specific, defined stages of long-term relationships, which offer new feelings, new challenges to overcome, and new opportunities for growth. And if you want your relationship to evolve into one of mutual respect, love and intimacy, it's likely that you'll have to experience all of the following relationship stages at some point or another. Take a look at the description of each phase - does any of this sound familiar?

Before we get started, you should know that most people experience these stages in this order, and will need to resolve the challenges in each stage before they can move successfully on to the next. Of course there are always exceptions to this rule. But for the most part, you can't get out of experiencing all of these stages if you want a healthy and fulfilling relationship. Every couple will move through these stages at different speeds, and most people will experience each stage more than once - it is common to fluctuate from one stage to another.*

---

[20] Sarah M. Schultz, MA, CPC. http://www.newheightslifecoaching.com

Okay, now that I've given you the basic info, let's dig a little deeper....

Stage 1 - The Romance Stage

This is also known as the COURTSHIP PHASE OR THE FANTASY STAGE, and can last anywhere from 2 months to 2 years. This is when you and your partner have just met, and everything is absolutely amazing. You can't get enough of each other. <u>Neither of you can do any wrong in the eyes of the other... mainly because you're both still on your best behavior. The focus in this stage is on commonalities - you have so many common interests, you could practically be the same person!</u> You show your partner your absolute best self, and you try to please each other as much as possible. Conflict is seen as "bad" in this stage, and is avoided at all costs. You can't imagine living without this person, so you begin spending as much time together as possible. This is the stage when our defenses are down the most, which allows you to be open to and fall in love. You and your partner are building an important foundation in this stage, so your relationship can grow. There are biological effects as well. When you're in this stage, your body is producing enormous amounts of endorphins, which makes you feel unusually happy, positive and excited about everything in your life (this is that "head over heels in love" feeling!). This is the stage most often portrayed in movies and romantic novels, for obvious reasons. Bottom line - you are happier than you've ever been, and can't imagine ever feeling any differently.

Stage 2 - The Disillusionment Stage

This stage is also known as the FAMILIARIZATION STAGE, OR THE ADJUSTING TO REALITY PHASE. This is where you begin to realize that your partner is actually a human being (horror of horrors!). <u>You get to know each other more and more, and as a result you start recognizing their various flaws and shortcomings. You see</u>

your partner in relaxed situations, and you become more relaxed as well. Since your body cannot possibly continue to produce the same levels of endorphins that it did in the beginning, those feelings of being on top of the world start to decline. Your partner's little habits aren't quite as cute as they used to be, but there is still enough goodwill from the Romance Stage that you're willing to overlook them. This stage can start to trickle into your relationship slowly, as you begin to see your partner for who s/he really is. Or sometimes it happens all of a sudden, when there has been some sort of dishonesty or deceit. This phase can be confusing and discouraging since you've just experienced so much openness and connection in the Romance Stage. **However, at this stage, your main job is to learn how to communicate and resolve conflict with this person effectively, which is an important skill if you want your relationship to continue.**

Stage 3 - The Power Struggle Stage

This stage is also known as the DISAPPOINTMENT PHASE OR DISTRESS STAGE. As the characteristics from the Disillusionment Phase intensify, they become harder and harder to deal with. You will most likely begin to pull away from each other in this stage. At this point, you both still believe that conflict is a "bad" thing, but you are increasingly aware of your many differences. You fight to draw boundaries in the relationship, and as a result even small annoyances become big issues. This is the stage where you define unacceptable behavior, and most couples have occasional or frequent thoughts of leaving the relationship. More and more often, you start to feel like your partner is self-centered or un-caring, or even worse, that they simply can't be trusted. Deep resentments begin to build if you're unable to resolve your issues in a respectful and mutually agreeable way. Many couples get stuck in this stage because this way of interacting becomes normal in their relationship. This is when it is absolutely necessary to learn to manage your differences effectively - to communicate and work together as a team, even though it's tempting to believe that your partner's sole purpose on Earth is to make your life difficult. Not surprisingly, this is the stage most couples are in when they decide to break up or file for divorce. However, if they are able to negotiate all of the landmines during this phase, they'll move on to....

Stage 4 - The Stability Stage

This is a restful and peaceful time, compared to the last stage. This stage is also known as the FRIENDSHIP PHASE OR RECONCILIATION STAGE. Some couples never make it to this stage, but the ones who do find that they have deeper feelings of love, connection and trust with their partner. You now have history together, and most people begin to rely on the predictability of the relationship. As you enter this stage, you begin to realize that your partner isn't perfect, but your personal differences aren't quite as threatening as they used to be. You're able to resolve most of your differences, at least to some extent, and you become more confident in the relationship. Some people feel a sense of loss in this stage as they learn to accept their partner for who they truly are. This means they have to let go of the fantasy that was established early on in the relationship. But for the most part, the deepening sense of friendship and commitment is a good trade-off for those early feelings of butterflies and excitement. This is also when you begin to re-establish your own outside interests and friendships, which were given up in the Romance Phase. There is some danger that you may begin to drift apart from or become bored with your partner in this phase, so you should try to maintain the connection that was created in the Romance Phase. Overall, this is the stage when you finally begin to feel comfortable and happy with your deepening relationship.

Stage 5 - The Commitment Stage

This stage is also known as the ACCEPTANCE PHASE, THE TRANSFORMATION STAGE, OR THE REAL LOVE PHASE. It is estimated that fewer than 5% of couples actually make it to this stage, according to The Relationship Institute. This is the stage when both couples have a clear notion of who their partner is, faults, foibles and weaknesses galore... yet they make a conscious choice to be with this person in spite of all of those things (and in some cases because of those things). <u>You are no longer with your partner because you need them, but because you've chosen them. This means the level of resentment you felt in the Power Struggle Phase has decreased, if not disappeared. If you've made it to this stage, you and your partner are a team.</u> You genuinely love your partner, and you look out for their best interests just as much as you look out for your own. Your partner is your best friend. There are few surprises about your partner's habits or character in this phase. You've collaborated to overcome many challenges together, and have grown to accept and support each other without restriction. Your vision for your relationship is in congruence with who you are and what you both truly want. You have discussed your future together - you have similar life goals, and you feel encouraged to define your relationship further. <u>Many couples decide to make a formal or public commitment to each other in this stage (such as marriage) to demonstrate their intention to continue their relationship. This is the stage in which your relationship becomes a true partnership.</u> **(Many people are married in the earlier phases but will still go through the processes).**

Appendix F

CHAPTER - Dew Tell BTR Show - Transcript
COMMUNICATION – "CAN YOU HEAR ME NOW?"

I. DEFINITIONS:

Communication is the activity of conveying information. Communication requires a **sender**, a **message**, and an **intended recipient**, although the receiver need not be present or aware of the sender's intent to communicate at the time of communication. Thus communication can occur across vast distances in time and space. Communication requires that the communicating parties share an area of communicative commonality. **The communication process is complete once the receiver _has understood_ the sender.**

Two-way process of reaching mutual understanding, in which participants not only exchange (encode-decode) information but also create and share meaning.

II. FOUR TYPES OF COMMUNICATION:

Communication of information, messages, opinions, speech and thoughts can be done via different forms of modern communication media, e.g., e-mail, telephone and mobile phone. Some of the basic ways of communication are by speaking, singing, sign language, body language, touch, and eye contact. These basic ways of communication are used to transfer information from one entity to other. There are many different modes or methods of communication but they can be classified into **four basic types** of communication. These four types of communication are as follows:

Verbal Communication

Verbal communication includes sounds, words, language, and speaking. Language is said to have originated from sounds and gestures. There are many languages spoken in the world. The bases of language formation are gender, class, profession, geographical area, age group, and other social elements. Speaking is an effective way of communicating and is again classified into two types, viz., interpersonal communication and public speaking.

Fluent verbal communication is essential to deal with people. Also in communication, self-confidence plays a vital role which when combined with fluent communication skills, can lead to success.

Public speaking is another verbal communication in which you have to address a group of people. Preparing for an effective speech before you start is important. In public speaking, the speech must be prepared according to the type of audience you are going to face.

Non-Verbal Communication

Non-verbal communication involves physical ways of communication like tone of the voice, touch, smell, and body motion. Body language is a non-verbal way of communication. Body posture and physical contact convey a lot of information. Body posture matters a lot when you are communicating verbally to someone. Folded arms and crossed legs are some of the signals conveyed by a body posture. Physical contact, like, shaking hands, pushing, patting, and touching expresses the feeling of intimacy. Facial expressions, gestures, and eye contact are all different ways of communication. Reading facial expressions can help you know a person better.

Written Communication

Written communication is writing the words which you

want to communicate. Good written communication is.

Visual communication

The last type of communication out of the four is the visual communication. Visual communication is visual display of information, like, topography, photography, signs, symbols, and designs. Television and video clips are the electronic form of visual communication.

I. BARRIERS TO COMMUNICATION

Different Types of Barriers in Communication

Language Barrier

This is one of the major barriers to communication that is faced in our personal lives as well as at the workplace. People might not be good at communicating in a particular language, which may eventually lead to a goof up in the message to be passed on.

Cultural Barrier

In our society nowadays people come from different countries, and hence different cultures. These differences in cultures may lead to one not communicating sufficiently or appropriately with other individuals from another culture. This is one of the barriers in intercultural communication.

Gender Barrier

According to some research, it has been found that women tend to talk much more as compared to men. Men talking less may sometimes prove to be a barrier to clear communication. In addition, men tend to talk direct and logical, whereas women's talk is usually mixed with emotions and logic.

Emotional Barrier

If you are not in a good mood or are disturbed due to a

problem in your personal or professional life, you happen to pay less attention in the communication cycle. This barrier to communication is evident when you have a conversation or interaction with someone, without knowing afterwards what was actually discussed. This is one of the barriers in interpersonal communication.

Physical Barrier
This is one of the very common barriers in a work or school setting, but can also play out in the home setting as well. At the workplace, the physical distance from the sender and receiver may make it difficult for the message to be passed on effectively, leading to inadequate communication. In the home, people may actually even try yelling at one another from different rooms only to learn later that some important parts of the conversation were actually not heard.

Presentational Barrier
If the way you present what you are saying is not good and clear and to the point, the message sent is not understandable. This may in turn lead to guess work among the participants. A good and well-planned presentation is very significant for effective communication.

One-way Communication Barrier
Good communication is roughly defined as one which has both the sender and the receiver involved. If the message is sent but there is no feedback about whether it was clearly received, it should be considered incomplete communication.

Listening Barrier
Another communication barrier is when the receiver does not or is unable to listen to your message. This is generally caused due to poor listening skills of the receiver. For this matter, professionals need to be active listeners instead of passive ones.

Stress Barrier
There are many times when you forget what the speaker

said or communicated. This is because you may be too tired and stressed out. Stress does lead to improper listening and participation and thus unclear communication.

Skills Barrier
In a setting like the Workplace or school, communication also depends much on the skill level of the listeners and the receivers of the message. If the listener does not possess the relevant skill about the topic which is being communicated, he is likely to not understand a thing.

Overcoming communication barriers is the most important task that has to be carried out in a process for it to be successful.

IV. POSITIVE SKILLS FOR HEALTHY RELATIONSHIPS:

Communication is a very crucial part of our lives, especially when it comes to relationships. In order for a relationship to run smoothly, there should be effective communication between both partners. This is why you need to include practicing communication skills in relationships. By improving communication skills in relationships, you will be able to understand the feelings of the other person clearly and effectively. Understanding the importance of communication skills in relationships will even help you prevent and overcome any misunderstanding between both partners

Effective Communication Skills in Relationships

Listen Carefully
There are many things that we mess up just because we fail to listen to what the other person actually is saying. This can even happen in a relationship. When communicating with your partner, don't just hear, but listen carefully. This will enable you to understand what the other person is saying and prepare for a response. During listening, do not

interrupt the other person. If you do so, it would naturally show your disinterest in the matter.

Speak

Just like careful listening; speaking clearly is also a very significant point when it comes to good communication skills in relationships. What you speak has to be balanced with what you have heard. Do not overstate what you want to say and be clear. While speaking, it is always better to consider the other person's point of view. Do not be rude or one-sided in your talk with your partner, and most importantly do not criticize.

Understand Body Language

Body language is another essential aspect of good communication in relationships. If you want to reach greater depths in understanding each other, you also need to use body language in your communication. Along with just plain listening and speaking, you also have to include body language as a part of your communication. This includes eye movements, posture, and other facial expressions. Good body language can be used in order to show interest in the communication.

Use the 'I' Word Correctly

The 'I' word plays a very important role when it comes to clear communication in relationships. Using 'I' in your statements gives an impression that what is being said is your point of view, and the views can differ. Instead of using the statement 'You make me frustrated', it is a good option to say, 'I don't like it when this happens'. This makes the conversation less accusatory and makes the other person feel that he is not being totally blamed.

Other Skills

You should communicate in a way that would create a kind

of mutual understanding between both partners. The communication should essentially lead to a solution and not more complications in the conflict. In some cases, physical touch can even contribute to good understanding in both partners. For instance, just holding hands while talking, can be of great help to pass on the message effectively.

It is also significant to accept that you are wrong if you really are. Learn to appreciate your partner to enhance the quality of your communication. Another good idea is to turn a complaint into a request by saying please and other such words. Instead of shouting 'You never say goodbye!' you can just say 'Can you please say goodbye while going?'

Appendix G

ANGER

Anger is a natural part of the human condition, but it isn't always easy to handle. When people don't handle it well, the harm they do can be visible or it can be not visible.

Some people mask their anger. Others explode with rage. For still others, anger is a chronic condition, a habit of resentment that surfaces over and over again.

There are ten primary anger styles:

Anger Avoidance: These people don't like anger much. Some are afraid of their anger or the anger of others. It can be scary, and they are afraid to lose control if they get mad. Some think it's bad to become angry. Anger avoiders gain the sense that being good or nice helps they feel safe and calm.

They have problems though. Anger can help you to survive when something is wrong. Avoiders can't be assertive because they feel too guilty when they say what they want. Too often the result is that they are walked over by others.

Sneaky Anger: Anger Sneaks never let others know they are angry. Sometimes they don't even know how angry they are. But the anger comes out in other forms, such as forgetting things a lot, or saying they'll do something, but never intending to follow through. Or they sit around and frustrate everybody and their families. Anger Sneaks can look hurt and innocent and often ask, "Why are you getting mad at me?" They gain a sense of control over their lives when they frustrate others. By doing little or nothing, or putting things off, they are thwarting other people's plans. However, Anger Sneaks lose track of their own wants and needs. They don't know what to do with their own lives and that leads to boredom, frustration, and unsatisfying relationships.

Paranoid Anger: This type of anger occurs when someone feels irrationally threatened by others. They seek aggression everywhere. They believe people want to take what is theirs. They expect others will attack them physically or verbally. Because of this belief, they spend much time jealously guarding and defending what they think is theirs - the love of a partner (real or imagined), their money or their valuables. People with Paranoid anger give their anger away. They think everybody else is angry instead of acknowledging their own rage. They have found a way to get angry without guilt. Their anger is disguised as self-protection. It is expensive though. They are insecure and trust nobody. They have poor judgment because they confuse their own feelings with those of others. They see their own anger in the eyes and words of their friends, mates, and co-workers. This leaves them (and everyone around them) confused.

Sudden Anger: People with sudden anger are like thunderstorms on a summer day. They zoom in from nowhere, blast everything in sight, and then vanish. Sometimes it's only lightning and thunder, a big show that soon blows away. But often people get hurt, homes are broken up, and things are damaged that will take a long time to repair. Sudden Anger people gain a surge of power. They release all their feelings, so they feel good or relieved. Loss of control is a major problem with sudden anger. They can be a danger to themselves and others. They may get violent. They say and do things they later regret, but by then it's too late to take them back.

Shame-Based Anger: People who need a lot of attention or are very sensitive to criticism often develop this style of anger. The slightest criticism sets off their own shame. Unfortunately, they don't like themselves very much. They feel worthless, less than good enough, broken, and unlovable. So, when someone ignores them or says something negative, they take it as proof that the other person dislikes them as much as they dislike themselves. But that makes them really angry so that they lash out. They think, "You made me feel awful, so I'm going to hurt you back." They get rid of their shame by blaming, criticizing, and ridiculing others. Their anger helps them get revenge against anybody they think shamed them. They avoid their own feelings of inadequacy by shaming others. Raging against others to hide shame doesn't work very well. They usually end up attacking the people they love. They continue to be oversensitive to insults because of their poor self-image. Their anger and loss of control only makes them feel worse about themselves.

Deliberate Anger: This anger is planned. People who use this anger usually know what they are doing. They aren't really emotional about their anger, at least not at first. They like controlling others, and the best way they've discovered to do that is with anger and violence, at times. Power and control are what people gain from deliberate anger. Their goal is to get what they want by threatening or overpowering others. This may work for a while, but this usually breaks down in the long run. People don't like to be bullied and eventually they figure out ways to escape or get back at the bully.

Addictive Anger: Some people want or need the strong feelings that come with anger. They like the intensity even if they don't like the trouble their anger causes them. Their anger is much more than a bad habit - it provides emotional excitement. It isn't fun, but it's powerful. These people look forward to the anger "rush" and the emotional "high." Anger addicts gain a sense of intensity and emotional power when they explode. They feel alive and full of energy. Addictions are inevitably painful and damaging. This addiction is no exception. They don't learn other ways to feel good, so they become dependent upon their anger. They pick fights just to get high on anger. Since they need intensity, their anger takes on an all-or-nothing pattern that creates more problems than it solves.

Habitual Anger: Anger can become a bad habit. Habitually angry people find themselves getting angry often and usually about small things that don't bother others. They wake up grumpy. They go through the day looking for fights. They look for the worst in everything and everybody. They usually go to bed angry about something. They might even have angry dreams. Their angry thoughts set them up for more and more arguments. They can't seem to quit being angry even though they are unhappy. Habitually angry people gain predictability. They always know what they feel. Life may be lousy, but it is known, safe, and steady. However, they get trapped in their anger and it runs their lives. They can't get close to the people they love because their anger keeps them away.

Moral Anger: Some people think they have a right to be angry when others have broken a rule. That makes the offenders bad, evil, wicked, and sinful. They have to be scolded and maybe punished. People with this anger style feel outraged about what bad people are doing. They say they have a right to defend their "beliefs." They claim moral superiority. They gain the sense that anger is for a good cause. Because of this, they don't feel guilty when they get angry. They often feel superior to others even in their anger. These people suffer from black-and-white thinking, which means they see the world too simply. They fail to understand people who are different from themselves. They often have rigid ways of thinking and doing things. Another problem with this anger style is crusading - attacking every problem or difference of opinion with moral anger when compromise or understanding might be better.

Hate: Hate is a hardened anger. It is a nasty anger style that happens when someone decides that at least one other person is totally evil or bad. Forgiving the other person seems impossible. Instead, the hater vows to despise the offender. Hate starts as anger that doesn't get resolved. Then it becomes resentment and then a true hatred that can go on indefinitely. Haters often think about the ways they can punish the OFFENDER and they sometimes act on those ideas. These people feel they are innocent victims. They create a world of enemies to fight, and they attack them with great vigor and enthusiasm. However, this hatred causes serious damage over time. Haters can't let go or get on with life. They become bitter and frustrated. Their lives become mean, small, and narrow.

Anger is a tricky emotion; difficult to use well until you learn how. It is a real help though, as long as you don't get trapped in any of the anger styles aforementioned. People who use anger well have a healthy or "normal" relationship with their anger. They think of anger in the following characteristic ways:

- Anger is a normal part of life
- Anger is an accurate signal of real problems in a person's life
- Angry actions are screened carefully. You needn't automatically get angry just because you could
- Anger is expressed in moderation so there is no loss of control
- The goal is to solve the problems, not just to express anger
- Anger is clearly stated in ways that others can understand
- Anger is temporary. It can be relinquished once an issue is resolved

When you practice good anger skills, you never need to use your anger as an excuse. You can take responsibility for what you say and do, even when you are mad.

The more you know about your personal anger style(s), the more control you will have over your life. You can learn to let go of excessive anger and resentment.

3) Overcoming Jealousy, Anger, and Need to Control

Overcoming jealousy is like changing any emotional reaction or behavior. It begins with awareness. Awareness allows you to see that the projected stories in your mind are not true. When you have this clarity, you no longer react to the scenarios that your mind imagines. Jealousy and anger are emotional reactions to believing scenarios in your mind that are not true. By changing what you believe, you change what your imagination is projecting, and you can eliminate these destructive emotional reactions. Even when there is justification for the reaction, jealousy and anger are not beneficial ways to deal with the situation and get what we want.

Trying to change anger or jealousy once you are in the emotion is like trying to control a car skidding on ice. Your ability to handle the situation is greatly improved if you can steer clear of the hazard before we get there. This means addressing the beliefs that trigger jealousy instead of attempting to control your emotions.

To permanently dissolve the emotions such as anger and jealousy in relationships means changing the core beliefs of insecurity and mental projections of what your partner is doing.

The steps to permanently end jealous reactions are:
1) **Recovering personal power** so that you can get control of your emotions and refrain from the reactive behavior.
2) **Shift your point of view** so that you can step back from the story in your mind. This will give you a gap of time in which to refrain from a jealous or angry reaction

and do something else.
3) **Identify the core beliefs** that trigger the emotional reaction.
4) **Become aware** that the beliefs in your mind are not true. This is different than "knowing" intellectually that the stories are not true.
5) **Develop control over your attention** so you can consciously choose what story plays in your mind and what emotions you feel.

There are a number of elements that create the dynamic of jealousy. As such, effective solutions will have to address multiple elements of beliefs, points of view, emotions, and personal will power. If you miss one or more of these elements, you leave the door open for those destructive emotions and behaviors to return.

By practicing a few simple exercises you can step back from the story your mind is projecting and refrain from the emotional reaction. If you really have the desire to change your emotions and behavior, you can do it. It just takes the willingness to learn effective skills.

Principle triggers of jealousy are beliefs that create feelings of insecurity.
Feelings of low self esteem are based in beliefs we have in a mental image of who we are. In order to eliminate the insecurity and low self esteem we don't have to change. We just have to change our belief in the false self image. While some people assume this may be hard, it is only challenging when people have not learned the skills necessary to change a belief. Once you practice the skills you find that changing a belief takes very little effort. You just stop believing the story in your mind. It takes more effort to believe something than it does to not believe it.

Self Judgment can amplify the feeling of insecurity
It is not enough to "know" intellectually that we are

creating the emotion. With only this information the Inner Judge is likely to abuse us with criticism for what we are doing. The Inner Judge might use this information to take us on an emotional downward spiral to further insecurity. For real lasting change you will need develop skills to dissolve the beliefs and false self images and gain control of what your mind projects. The practices and skills are available in the audio sessions. Session 1 and 2 are free sessions and should lend insight into how the mind works to create emotions. Session 1 and 2 also give you excellent exercises to recover some personal power and begin shifting your emotions.

One of the steps to changing a behavior is to see how we actually create the emotion of anger or jealousy from the images, beliefs, and assumptions in our mind. This step not only allows us to take responsibility, but taking responsibility for our emotions also puts us in a position of power to change them.

If you are in a relationship with a jealous partner and they want you to change your behavior to prevent the jealousy, then they are not taking responsibility. If they say things like, "If you wouldn't _____, then I wouldn't react this way." That type of language flags an attitude of powerlessness and an attempt to control your behavior with a deal.

How the mind creates the emotions of jealousy and anger

I've outlined the dynamics of jealousy and anger in the explanation below. If you are seeking to overcome jealousy, it is likely that you already know the dynamics that I describe. This description may help fill in some gaps of how the mind twists knowledge into self judgment and reinforces low self esteem and insecurity. This intellectual understanding can help develop awareness to see these dynamics in the moment you are doing them. But to really make effective changes you will need a different skill set. Knowing how you create your emotional reactions doesn't give you enough information about how to change them. Just like knowing you got a flat tire because you ran over a nail doesn't mean you know how to patch the tire.

For the illustration I'll use a man as the jealous partner. I refer to various images in the mind and you can use the diagram below for reference.

It starts with a man feeling insecure about him. Insecurity comes from his False Hidden Image of being "not good enough". With the belief that this false image is him rather than an image in his mind, the man creates self rejection in his mind. The emotional result of self rejection is a feeling of unworthiness, insecurity, fear, and unhappiness.

Compensating for Insecurity
In order to overcome the emotion generated from his Hidden False Image, he focuses on his perceived positive qualities. From these qualities the man creates a more positive False Image of himself. I call this the Projected Image because this is how he wants to be seen. The emotional result of a positive self image is no self rejection and no feeling of unworthiness. There is greater acceptance for him; therefore he creates more love and happiness. Notice that he has not changed, he is just holding on to a different image in his mind depending on the moment.

The Hidden Image beliefs become the triggers of unhappiness while the Projected Image triggers more pleasant emotions. It is important to note that both images are false. Both images are in the man's mind and neither one is really him. He is the one that is creating and reacting to the images in his imagination. He is not an image in his imagination.

The man's mind associates the Projected Image with qualities women are attracted to. Often the qualities are considered positive as a result of the assumption that women are attracted to them. When the man gets attention from a woman, he associates himself with the Projected Image rather than the "Not Good Enough" image. The strengthened belief in the Projected Image results in more self acceptance, love, and happiness in his emotional state.

It is the man's action of acceptance and love that changes his emotional state. It is not the image or the woman's attention that change his emotion. These are only triggers that activate the man's mind towards certain beliefs, self acceptance, and love.

The man's mind often makes the false assumption that "she makes him happy" or that he "needs" her to be happy. It only appears this way because he is noticing the woman's relationship to his emotional state. Often the man doesn't realize that she is just an emotional trigger for his mind to express love. He may not have formed other triggers for expressing his own acceptance and love, so he is dependent on a woman for a trigger. When the man recognizes that she is only a trigger, and his role of expressing acceptance and love is what changes his emotional state, then the man doesn't "need" his partner in order to be happy.

The man's conflicting False Images might look like this in his mind.

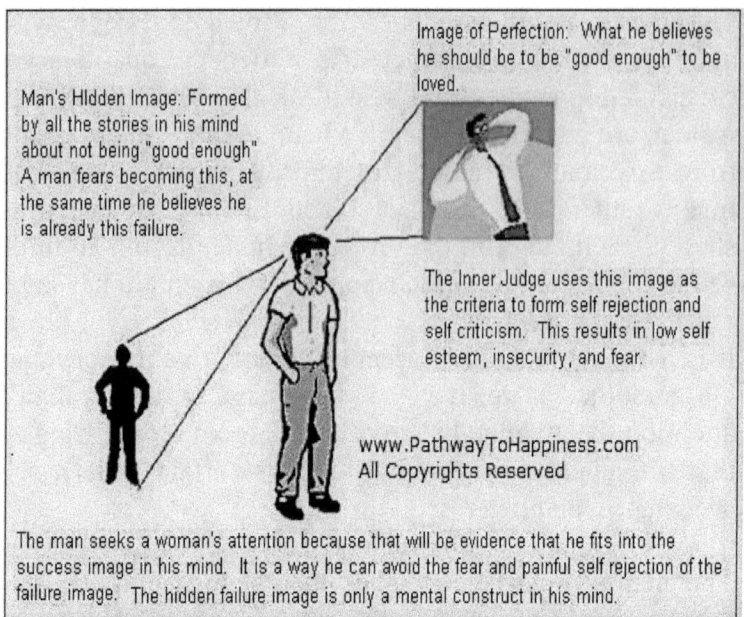

Controlling Behavior

The man is operating from the false belief that he is happier because of a woman's attention and love. When he imagines that her attention is on someone or something other than himself, he reacts with fear. The majority of the fear is not about losing the woman as he might falsely believe. The majority of the fear is about avoiding the emotional pain he creates in his mind with the Hidden Image.

Without her attention, his Hidden Image beliefs become active. His point of view about himself also moves into perceiving from this "not good enough" state. His emotion of unworthiness and unhappiness follows his paradigm of beliefs and point of view.

The man attempts to get and control the woman's attention so that the Projected Image beliefs are active. He works to "activate" her "trigger" to support his Projected Image beliefs. It is the mechanism he knows for avoiding his emotionally unpleasant Hidden Image beliefs. He is not aware that it is the expression of love and acceptance that is the means to change his emotional state.

Anger and punishment to control behavior
One of the mechanisms we learn early in life is to control other people's attention and behavior through the emotion of anger. When we were punished as children, anger often accompanied that punishment. Sometimes just harsh words were enough to get us to change a behavior. At a very minimum when someone was angry at us, it got our attention. In this way we learned early in life to use anger as a means to control other people's attention, and as a punishment to control behavior. As we got older, we didn't necessarily unlearn this pattern.

The jealous man uses anger towards his partner in order to get and control her attention. Anger also works as a punishment with the result of inflicting emotional pain on the woman. By punishing the woman with anger the woman may change her behavior in order to avoid emotional punishment in the future.

The man's use of anger may not be his preferred choice. But his behavior of anger is the result of a false belief paradigm. The man may "know" differently at the level of his intellect, but his behavior is based in the false beliefs and Hidden Image that push his emotions.

The actual result of Controlling Anger
With his anger the man gets the opposite result that he was conditioned to get as a child. An adult generally has more power to resist the punishment of anger than does a child. The woman will withdraw from him because of her tendency to avoid the emotionally unpleasant. Her withdrawal will then activate his Hidden Image beliefs that he was working to avoid. The man's belief-emotion cycle returns to the beginning. This is emotionally painful.

The Analysis after the Incident

After a jealousy and anger incident, there is an opportunity to look at and analyze the events. For the jealous man, this time can often be more painful emotionally. This is when his self judgment can be at its worst.

The man plays over in his mind the behavior of anger and control. However, now it is reviewed from the viewpoint of the Inner Judge in his mind. The Inner Judge does the analysis and condemns him. The Inner Judge specifically holds up the Projected Image and then points out that "he failed" to live up to that standard. Based on the Projected Image standard he can only conclude he is a failure and not good enough. .

The anger incident, when viewed by the Inner Judge is "evidence" that he is actually the person that fits the Hidden Image description. Accepting and believing this judgment results in the man feeling unworthiness, guilt, and shame. The belief, emotion, and point of view of the Hidden Image character is reinforced

The Inner Judge does not give the man a fair trial. It is a hanging Judge. The Inner judge does not assess the role of the Belief System, the False Images or the Point of View. The man is at the mercy of forces in his mind that he has not been trained to see and deal with. With awareness of these forces and some specific practice he can begin to get control over his emotional state.

This chain reaction happens very fast
The man has gone through an array of emotions and self images in his mind, usually very quickly. Often the process happens so fast that he is not aware of what the mind and belief system has done. Also, the denial system pushes his mind toward not acknowledging the Hidden Image as that would be too painful emotionally. Because

of the multiple elements of the reaction, it is easy to miss critical elements such as point of view and assumptions of how emotion is created. Missing these critical elements distorts our conclusions and makes our efforts to change ineffective.

Efforts to change behavior don't seem to work
The principle problem in the analysis is that the man studies the events from the point of view of judgment. Judgment adds to the rejection. It also operates to reinforce the belief in the standard of Perfection. This point of view reinforces the Hidden Image, and the Projected Image beliefs which are part of the core cause. The very part of our mind that is doing the analysis is actually reinforcing the core causes.

The man is looking for a solution, and in this paradigm of unworthiness, the solution looks like he should become the "Projected Image." If he can become the confident, strong, kind, and loving person he "knows" he is, then he will like himself and the woman will love him, and everything will be fine. He does not see that the Projected Image is formed in his imagination.

There are other problems with this approach.
1. The man's belief that he is the Projected Image is undermined by his belief that he is not "good enough." The Hidden Image beliefs create the feeling of unworthiness. Being perfect may compensate at times, but the feeling of unworthiness will seep through until the Hidden image is dealt with.

2. Even when the man pulls off being the perfect Projected Image, the Hidden Image beliefs will have part of him feeling like a fraud. According to the Hidden image beliefs, he is not really "Perfect", and he is not "Worthy." He will feel inauthentic because of these conflicting beliefs. The feeling of being a fraud often

happens when his successes are being praised by others. The more success and recognition he receives that fits the Projected Image, the more pronounced the Hidden Image push up doubts in his mind.

He cannot be in Emotional Integrity as long as he associates his identity with one or more conflicting images in his mind.

3. The man's efforts at controlling his emotion will have him continually on guard against an outburst of jealousy and anger. This "on guard" feeling is born out of fear that at any moment he may fall, and emotion will overtake his attention. This feeling of fear not only wears on a person, but represses emotion and doesn't allow for feeling authentic Love and Happiness.

4. Building strong positive beliefs and a positive self image can help to diminish the reaction side, but to a limited extent. It is a patch that can help for some but still bases identity in a false image and not in authenticity and integrity. It does not do anything to address the emotions that come from the Hidden Images or beliefs of unworthiness that are at the core of the behavior. These often become buried in the sub-conscious and resurface later during times of stress when they are most destructive, and we are least able to deal with them.

Emotion and False Beliefs Drive the Behavior
When one looks at the behavior of jealousy and anger as a means to control and keep someone, the behavior doesn't make sense. Anger and jealousy will not endear someone to be closer to us. The man in the situation can often look at his own behavior and see that it doesn't make sense. He can see the woman withdraw from him as a result of his behavior. Yet seeing the result and knowing this intellectually does not change the dynamics of his behavior. Why?

His behavior is not driven by thinking, logic or intellectual knowing. Therefore it cannot be changed by these modalities. It is driven by Beliefs, False Images, Point of View, and Emotion. If we are to change our behavior, we must address these fundamental elements in a manner different than plain intellect and logic. Why use an approach different than intellect and logic? The Inner Judge will use intellect and logic to create judgments and reinforce the existing false beliefs.

A Path with Results

The changing of beliefs, emotional reactions, and destructive behaviors is done through mastering your point of view and attention, and dissolving the false beliefs in your mind. When you learn to shift your Point of View, you can literally move yourself out of a Belief and out of an emotion. From a new point of view you will have the awareness to see the faulty logic of the beliefs behind the behavior. With the awareness of the false beliefs behind your actions you will be able to refrain from destructive behavior. Eliminating the false beliefs eliminates the triggers of your emotions. It is the elimination of the false beliefs that will dissolve the fear.

If you have enough desire to change a jealous and angry behavior, you will eventually have to do more than study the problem. You will have to take action.

Appendix H

"SEXUALITY AND SPIRITUALITY"

Transcript from "Dew Tell" Blog Talk Radio Show

For the sake of this discussion, I want to share two very, very general definitions:

Sexuality: *Generally speaking, human "sexuality" is how people experience and express themselves as sexual beings. The study of human sexuality encompasses an array of social activities, an abundance of behaviors, series of actions, and societal norms or boundaries.*

Spirituality: *The definition of "spirituality" is that which relates to or affects the human spirit or soul as opposed to material or physical things. Spirituality touches that part of you that is not dependant on material things or physical comforts.*

Over the last few weeks, we have talked primarily about the actual anatomy and physiology of the human sexual organs. "Anatomy" has to do with identifying and naming the various body parts and organs, while "physiology" has to do with the actual function or purpose of those body parts and organs. We have progressed from the moment of conception through development in the womb, through childhood, and into puberty. Puberty includes the drastic physical, emotional, psychological, and etc., changes that take place as the person transitions out of childhood into early adulthood. Now I am going to take a shift out of the primary physical aspect of sexuality. As we move into adulthood, there is another aspect of our lives that immensely impacts upon our self concept in relationship to our sexuality. There is absolutely no way that we can cover every aspect of the connection between sexuality and spirituality on tonight's show, and probably not even within a few months' worth of Dew Tell Shows.

Therefore I would like to make a statement up front to share what my primary focus is as I begin a limited discussion of this joint subject. I wholeheartedly believe that it is high time that the subject of sexuality be taken out of the gutter where negative forces within our society insist on taking it, along with the morals and values of our young people and many adults. It is time for people who believe in the creation of humankind by a loving and reverent God, to bring back awareness within our society that every area of our lives, our bodies, our souls, our spirits, our emotions, and our genitalia were created for a good purpose. Not to sound too preachy, I just firmly believe that no amount of fussing, punishment, condoms, birth control or whatever else adults use to try to bring the horse back into the stable - once it has gotten out and gone buck wild will help, without us retraining our children to think of their whole self as precious and of value, and not deserving of slutty behavior, actions and abuse. Unless our daughters know that their bodies are a wondrous gift which they are to treat with care – they won't understand why they should not wear clothes that expose their body to every human eye that comes into contact with them, and every Tom, Jack, and Harry that gives them a smile. If we don't teach our young men that they were created as vessels of honor, they won't understand why they should not relieve their seed in every female that they can beguile, and that your body parts have great value and worth to the God who created us for Himself and for one another.

Having said that, I would like to go to the instruction manual which informs us of "how" and "why" we were made. Also, it tells us how we should function effectively in this seeing, touching, smelling, feeling and hearing body. Fact of the matter is the genitalia are not the only part of the human body which responds to the sight, smell or touch of another human being. Our entire body is created to react to another human being. That's what gives us the ability to receive and express love and affection – notice I did not say "lust", but love.

One of the most powerful and profound aspects of any relationship is emotion. If we learn to maintain healthier emotions, we can change all of our relationships.

Appendix I

SEXUAL DEVELOPMENT[21] - FYI

(Disclaimer – We may not agree with everything, but at least begin an open and honest dialogue with your young people. No more "cabbage patch" and "storks")

– September Summer

Sexual Development

I. Child sexuality

In the past, children were often assumed not to have sexuality until later development. Sigmund Freud was one of the first researchers to take child sexuality seriously. Ongoing research has helped to validate many of his ideas. Freud demonstrated that sexual drives do exist and can be discerned in children from birth. His position further stated that sexual energy (libido) becomes the single most important motivating force in adult life. Freud wrote about the importance of interpersonal relationships to ones sexual and emotional development. From the initial days of life, the mother's physical and emotional connection to the infant has an effect on the infant's later capacity for pleasure and attachment. Further research has also demonstrated that where there is little to no physical touch during infancy and early childhood, there will be challenges with being able to develop emotionally and intimately healthy relationships with others in adulthood.

---

[21] Bell, R. "Changing Bodies, *Changing Lives: A Book for Teens on Sex and Relationships*. New York: Random House, 1988

Freud described two currents of emotional life in all of us: (1) an affectionate current, including our bonds with the important people in our lives, and (2) a sensual current, including our wish to gratify sexual impulses. During adolescence, a young person tries to integrate these two emotional currents. This is a difficult task as the parent of any teenager can tell you. There are numerous inner conflicts and failures of development that may keep a person repeating immature sexual patterns. This is evident in much that we see on the news and in the young people walking around with their body half exposed, and the high number of teenage pregnancies. The real challenge is to bring about a healthy merging and development of these two currents: <u>the affectionate and the sensual</u> in a spiritually, mentally, emotionally, socially, and physically appropriate way. The sexual "over excitement" often characteristic of adolescent experimentation is not appropriate or acceptable in a grown adult. During the formative years, and even in the midst of raging hormones, it is the responsibility of the adults to help these young people make it through their Rites of Passage with love, understanding, spiritual guidance and some definite boundaries. As a Christian, I very, very strongly believe that it is also the spiritual leader's and church's responsibility to help provide support and education to the young people, as well as to the parents. It is not helpful to anyone to just allow happenstance to govern our children's perception of their sexuality or what is right or wrong.

The fact of the matter is that from infancy throughout the senior years, sexual development and/or changes are taking place within the human body, including all types of responses to feelings, and later to include thoughts and actions. It was God the creator who created within humans all of the body parts, hormones, tactile nerves, and apparatus which enables us to experience pleasure from touch and affection. The question is not **_whether_** we are sexual beings, the real question is how, when, where, and with whom are we to share that part of our selves. That's why the need for correct boundaries and education should begin in childhood; for example -Don't scream in utter disgust and try to beat the young child to death for touching his or her private parts, or threaten him with Hell or insanity. Don't accuse the 2-year-old or the 5-year-old of being a little pervert, and think in *your* mind that they have visualized the whole act of sexual intercourse in their mind – that's in your mind, not theirs. Get some books which are age appropriate and start explaining how God created us to love and to be loved, but that there are also some boundaries involved, and that there is a time and season for certain activities - and it won't make you a freak of nature if you learn how to DISCIPLINE yourself in the sexual area of your life just like you have to do with other areas of your life, such as spending, eating, and etc. Don't make "sex" out to be an accident alien of nature that came from outer space to destroy the human race by making us all filthy, dirty and vulgar creatures. Also, don't spend hours and hours of time talking about it, making it ___the___ most important issue in life – some things are better handled in small doses over a period of time.

Freud's work led him to establish the stages of psychosexual development where he describes infantile sexuality through steps.[12] From the moment of birth an infant is driven in their actions by the desire for bodily and sexual pleasure. This is seen by Freud as the desire to release mental energy. At first, infants gain such release, and derive pleasure from the act of sucking. Freud terms this the oral stage of development. It's followed by a stage in which the center of pleasure or energy release is the anus, mainly in the act of defecation. This is termed the anal stage. Then, the young child develops an interest in its genitalia as a site of pleasure known as the phallic stage. According to Freud, the child then develops a deep sexual attraction for the parent of the opposite sex, and a hatred of the parent of the same sex. This is known as the Oedipus complex. However, this gives rise to socially derived feelings of guilt in the child, who eventually recognizes that it can never supersede the stronger parent. A male child also perceives himself to be at risk, he fears that if he persists in pursuing the sexual attraction for his mother, he may be harmed by the father. Both the attraction for the mother and the hatred are usually repressed, and the child typically resolves the conflict of the Oedipus complex by coming to identify with the parent of the same sex. This happens at the age of five, whereupon the child enters a latency period in which sexual motivations become much less pronounced. This lasts until puberty when mature genital development begins and the pleasure drive refocuses around the genital area.[13] Freud believed that this is the progression in normal human development, and is to be observed beginning at the infant level. The instinctual attempts to satisfy the pleasure drive are frequently checked by parental control and social influencing. For the child, the developmental process is in essence a movement through a series of conflicts. The successful resolution of these conflicts is crucial to adult mental health. Many mental illnesses, particularly hysteria, Freud held, can be traced back to unresolved conflicts experienced at this stage, or to events which otherwise disrupt the normal pattern of infantile development. For example, homosexuality is seen by some Freudians as resulting from a failure to resolve the conflicts of the Oedipus complex, particularly a failure to identify with the parent of the same sex. The obsessive concern with washing and personal hygiene which characterizes the behavior of some neurotics is seen as resulting from unresolved conflicts or repressions occurring at the anal stage.[13]

Alfred Kinsey also examined child sexuality in his Kinsey Reports. He concluded that children are naturally curious about their bodies and sexual functions. For example, they wonder where babies come from, they notice the differences between males and females, and many engage in genital play (often mistaken for masturbation). Child sex play includes exhibiting or inspecting the genitals. Many children take part in some sex play, typically with siblings or friends.[Sex play with others usually decreases as children go through their elementary school years, yet they still may possess romantic interest in their peers. Curiosity levels remain high during these years, but it is not until adolescence that the main surge in sexual interest occurs. Unfortunately, some of Kinsey's research was found to be unethical and immoral because they exploited the natural curiosity that children have about their bodies and permitted some illegal acts between adults and children.

II. *Puberty - a normal stage of life during which adolescents experience many physical, cognitive, and emotional changes.*

A. Few comments:

"Mostly I'm pretty scared because I don't know if I'm normal or, you know, just strange. My body seems to be changing but not like some of my friends. I still look pretty much like a little kid and my best friend looks like he's 18 or something. I don't want to go near the gym anymore because then I'll have to take a shower. I know the other guys are going to laugh at me because I, well, you know, just don't look developed."—John, age 13.

"Now I have zits all over my face, my nose is too big, and my breasts are too small. It really bothers me. I don't think guys will ever notice me, let alone like me if my body stays like this—I'm a disaster."—Dominique, age 14.

"No one had told me anything about menstruation. When I started to bleed and nobody was at home, I got so scared I called 911."—Aisha, age 12.

> **B.** During adolescence the body a child has had for several years seems to become different and sometimes strange. This phase of development is referred to as puberty and involves rapid changes in the body, including sexual maturation. Bodies change, attitudes about self and others change, thinking abilities change, and interest in sexual activities changes as well. The good news is that puberty does not last forever—most people get through it by age 18. During this period there are major physical and emotional changes associated with sexual development. This time is called puberty.

Puberty is the growth stage in which the reproductive organs mature. Girls begin puberty, on average, about two years before boys. For girls, the body changes associated with puberty usually begins between the ages of 8 and 13. For boys, the normal age range for the start of puberty is between 10 and 14. What starts puberty is unknown, but the hypothalamus, a small area located deep within the brain, plays a key role. During puberty the hypothalamus and pituitary gland, a pea-sized organ located just beneath the hypothalamus, send out chemical messages that cause the gonads, or sex glands (testes in boys, ovaries in girls), to increase production of sex hormones * (testosterone in boys and estrogen in girls). With the increase in these hormones, the body begins to develop "secondary" sex characteristics (body hair, breasts, deeper voice, and etc.) as well as to undergo a growth spurt.

Different cultures have different rites of passage to mark the milestones in an individual's sexual development. The organs involved in sexual reproduction also enlarge and develop. For girls this series of changes leads to menstruation and signals that the body is capable of sexual reproduction, or having babies. For boys these changes lead to the production of sperm. While boys may have experienced erections throughout childhood - ejaculation, which is the release of sperm in fluid called semen, is only possible when this developmental level has been achieved. During this process, many young guys begin to experience what is called "wet dreams", which is actually their body going through the erection-ejaculation process while the kid is asleep. These are also called nocturnal emissions. Nocturnal emissions are usual and normal for boys.

Uneducated parents have been known to unfairly beat or punish or criticize young men when the evidence shows up on the sheets – when the kid has no control over the process.

If a boy's pajamas or sheets are wet and sticky when he wakes up, he has probably had a wet dream. Sometimes a full bladder may cause an erection, so it is not uncommon for males to awaken with an erection. Because there are many ways to excite the penis to erection, sometimes men have erections for no apparent reason, or even at inconvenient times. Boys may have erections at times that can be embarrassing, perplexing, or even anxiety provoking. While it may seem embarrassing and troublesome, it is all quite normal. Talk – love – listen – talk – love – listen –talk – love - listen

Unfortunately, there are many studies which continue to show that neither girls nor boys are prepared for the physical changes that make their bodies seem strange and foreign. Most girls report they knew little if anything about what usually is referred to as a "period" before their first experience. It also is typical for boys not to understand their newly acquired potential for ejaculation. Menstruation and ejaculation can be very shocking and frightening experiences if one is unaware and unprepared. Pay attention to your children and begin to teach them little by little.

On top of the physical changes, adolescents also experience changes in mood, thinking, and in social interests. Most parents of teenagers start wondering who this stranger is. I want to speak briefly about the "normal" changes, even though they may seem schizoid to the parents.

Mood Swings

Changes in hormones in the adolescent body can trigger sudden and unpredictable changes in moods. One minute a boy or girl may be laughing and then, for no apparent reason, he or she can suddenly become angry or tearful. The different feelings that adolescents experience often make them feel like their emotions are on a roller coaster. The increased production of sex hormones is just one of many factors that contribute to these mood swings.

Cognition or Mental Changes

During this stage of life, adolescents develop the ability to think in more abstract and logical ways. They have a greater ability to examine their own, as well as others, thoughts. These improved cognitive abilities often contribute to the disagreements between adults and adolescents as the adolescent is trying out new ways of thinking about issues and the world. If adults are not prepared for the changing nature of the adolescent's thought process, then the adolescent may feel as if he or she is being misunderstood or "treated like a child." Similarly, when adolescents are just beginning to develop these different cognitive abilities, there may be times when they want to think and act more like their younger selves. The adults around them need to respond to these changes and provide appropriate, challenging opportunities, but not opportunities that will overwhelm or frustrate the adolescent. The adults surrounding the adolescent are also learning about this changing, new person and are undergoing a "development" process, too!

Sensitivity or Emotional Changes

Adolescents are also changing the way they think about themselves and others. Adolescents at this developmental stage are quite involved with their own thoughts and feelings. Many adolescents believe that everyone is as absorbed with himself or herself as he or she is. Additionally, adolescents at this time believe that others are looking at them or thinking about them in a critical manner. This may cause some adolescents to be very sensitive about body image, minor mistakes they make, or differences between themselves and others. Sometimes people refer to adolescents as "hyper-sensitive," which means that others feel that adolescents care too much about relatively minor things. For the adolescents, however, this hypersensitivity is part of the normal process of developing an understanding of who they are.

Uniqueness

Adolescents have a new sense of personal uniqueness or "egocentrism." At this stage, adolescents believe that no one else can ever understand how they feel, not parents or even friends. Sometimes, to maintain a sense of personal uniqueness, adolescents may have ideas and beliefs that seem inaccurate or unrealistic. This is a normal reaction to the changes that the adolescent is undergoing.

Invulnerability

Sometimes adolescents feel they are indestructible or invulnerable to danger. This can lead to reckless behaviors such as drug use, fast driving, "daredevil" behaviors, suicidal thoughts, or sexual promiscuity. The adolescent may be unable to comprehend accurately the potential risks and negative outcomes of these reckless acts. This is another area of potential conflict between adolescents and adults: adults are responsible for keeping adolescents safe, and adolescents perceive adult actions to be overly controlling, overly cautious, or "out of touch."

What About Sex?

Adolescent development comes with many new and different physical and emotional feelings. Some of the most confusing may be the sexual thoughts that cause sensations or reactions in the body. ***Both girls and boys experience***

sexual feelings. To the teenager, these feelings are pleasurable and exciting and perfectly normal. Sometimes it is difficult to understand what one is expected to do with these new sexual feelings. Adolescents are aware that adults and the society in which they live have many, often conflicting, ideas about sex. For example, even though masturbation is a normal part of human sexuality, many people feel embarrassed to talk about it or may feel it is harmful or sinful. Adults are important resources that can help adolescents learn that sexual development and the physical changes of their bodies are normal. Unfortunately many adults are reluctant to discuss these issues, and adolescents are left with the impression that there is something wrong or shameful about the natural functioning of their bodies. Talk – love- patience- talk – love – patience – talk- love- patience!!!! If you don't talk to them ahead of time and during the transition time, someone else will. The conclusions they come to usually are a mixture of truth and error.

Menstruation

When girls reach a particular stage of development, usually between ages 9 and 15, menstruation (MEN-stru-A-shun) begins. Every month a female's body readies for a possible pregnancy. Talk – love- prepare her – talk-love- prepare her – talk –love – prepare her. It's not "the curse" -

menstruation is a normal and important fact of a woman's life.

It is important for girls to be told about the various physical and emotional changes surrounding menstruation. For example, it is common for a woman's breasts to feel swollen and tender before her period begins. Other women experience temporary weight gain of a few pounds or sudden cravings for carbohydrates such as chocolate prior to their periods. Some women feel they are absent-minded or disorganized or that their emotions are out of control before their periods begin. Many women experience cramps, pains in the lower abdominal area, at the start of their periods. All of these experiences are normal, and it is important that young women are aware of these potential feelings as a natural part of menstruation.

Erections and Ejaculation

When boys reach puberty, they may begin to experience more frequent erections. Erections occur when blood rushes into the penis, causing it to grow and stiffen. Ejaculations occur when sperm mixes with fluids from a gland called the prostate gland, and exits through the opening of the penis. It is through ejaculation that sperm leaves the male's body to enter the female's body when they combine during sexual intercourse to begin a pregnancy. Not all erections lead to ejaculations or sexual intercourse. As boys mature, they may also have erections and orgasms during sleep or pleasurable dreams. These are often called "wet dreams" or nocturnal emissions. Nocturnal emissions are usual and normal for boys. If a boy's pajamas or sheets are wet and sticky upon awakening, he has probably had a wet dream. Sometimes a full bladder may cause an erection, so it is not uncommon for males to awaken with an erection. Because there are many ways to excite the penis to erection, sometimes men have erections for no apparent reason, or even at inconvenient times. Boys may have erections at times that can be embarrassing, perplexing, or even anxiety provoking. While it may seem embarrassing and troublesome, it is all quite normal. Discussing these confusing moments with someone the young man trusts and is comfortable with can help to reassure him about these experiences.

Masturbation

Masturbation is the self-stimulation of the genitals to achieve pleasurable sensations, sometimes resulting in sexual orgasm. It is one of the most common human sexual expressions. Children from about the age of 2 1/2 may masturbate. A recent study has shown that one-third of females and two-thirds of males report masturbating before they reached adolescence. Many parents are hesitant to condone or express their approval of masturbation. Many religions feel that masturbation is improper. It is a difficult topic to discuss openly even though the majority of teenage boys and girls report having masturbated by the end of puberty. It becomes a matter of personal choice, guided by one's beliefs and values. Next week, in our final segment on this topic, we'll deal with this a little more as we talk about sexuality and spirituality.

Pregnancy

Pregnancy is a natural outcome of sexual intercourse, unless through some other form of in vitro fertilization. Unless an adult couple is prepared and ready to start a family, an unexpected pregnancy can cause many problems. This is one of the reasons it is so important to consider the consequences of acting on one's sexual desires before engaging in intercourse. The only truly effective method of contraception, and the only one that is 100 percent effective, is to refrain from all sexual intercourse until ready for marriage and pregnancy. This is sometimes called "abstinence." We'll also talk more about this next week.

Sexually transmitted diseases

Although the use of condoms can decrease the risk, abstaining from intercourse or other risky sexual activities is the *only sure way* to prevent the spread of HIV/AIDS, gonorrhea, chlamydia, syphilis, herpes, and other sexually transmitted diseases. Many young people contract STDs and don't take it seriously until they get married, only to learn that they cannot have children.

Gender and/or Sexual Orientation

"Gender" has to do with who you are based on your DNA, chromosomes and genitalia, while "Sexual orientation" refers to one's feelings for and sexual attraction to other people. In our current society, the "new normal" says "People can be heterosexual, homosexual, or bisexual, and still be normal and sexually healthy." We'll look more closely at this also on next week, as well as sexuality in adulthood.

Resources

Books

Bell, R. *Changing Bodies, Changing Lives: A Book for Teens on Sex and Relationships.* New York: Random House, 1988.

Recommended Reading/Resources

1) "Healing For Damaged Emotions" by *David A. Seamands*

2) "Changes That Heal" by *Dr. Henry Cloud*

3) "Boundaries" by *Dr. Henry Cloud, Dr. John Townsend*

4) "Understanding the Purpose and Power of Woman" by *Dr. Myles Munroe*

5) "Women With Wind In Their Wings" by *Rev. Dr. M. Frances Manning-Fontaine*

6) "Driven by Destiny" by *Dr. LaVerne Adams*

7) "Destined To Reign" by *Joseph Prince*

8) "Reposition Yourself" by *T.D. Jakes*

9) "Healed Without Scars" by *Bishop David G. Evans*

10) "Who Switched Off My Brain: Control-ling Toxic Thoughts" by *Dr. Caroline Leaf*

Divorce Care Group - *www.divorcecare.com*
Celebrate Recovery - *www.celebraterecovery.com*

www.ingramcontent.com/pod-product-compliance
Lightning Source LLC
LaVergne TN
LVHW051550070426
835507LV00021B/2513